To Da

you are unstoppable !

DARE TO MAKE A DIFFERENCE

SUCCESS 101

<u>FOR TEENS</u>

JOHN A. ANDREWS

NATIONAL BESTSELLING AUTHOR

Published in the U.S.A. by
BooksThatWillEnhanceYourLife.com

A L I
Andrews Leadership International
www.AndrewsLeadershipInternational.com

ISBN: 9780983141945
Cover Design: John A. Andrews
Cover Photo: Anthony Johnson
Cover Graphics: Abhai Kaul
Edited by: Anne Shoemaker

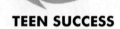

TEEN SUCCESS

This book is dedicated to my three sons, Jonathan 15, Jefferri 13 and Jamison 12. The trio has filled my life with drive and purpose, thereby enhancing my entire scope for the future. YOU keep me blazing the trails... I love YOU and I am proud of YOU!

-Dad.

Table of Contents

AUTHOR'S PREFACE

I'm writing this book for *teens* because:

1. I have two teenage sons and another soon to enter adolescence, and want all teens to be given the information/tools necessary to become successful .
2. I'm passionately embarking on a significant adventure; looking for teenagers who are willing to dare "walls" getting in the way of their vocation.
3. Our world needs young adults, who are willing to step off the sidelines and into the game – making a difference, to be successful and contributing citizens in the world.

I've discovered that most people in their early twenties to mid thirties don't really know what they want – they are dreamless. Evidently they have lived some of their greatest years without laying the proper foundation that will/can lead them to creating massive success in life.

In addition, several women in their late twenties have told me that it's hard finding a guy in his thirties who possess a success mindset and philosophy. They want a guy who can solve problems because in life whether you like it or not, you are either going through a problem, embarking on a problem, or wrapping up a problem. That's the way it is! This decline of a prepared generation has led me to believe that somewhere our society has dropped the ball. Yes, when it comes to preparing our youngsters for massive success and if it's not picked up soon enough - future generations could wind up immersed in that deficit.

I read my first book on personal development *The Magic of Thinking Big* almost 25 years ago when I was---. I'll tell you it has made a significance difference in my whole mindset and philosophy - when it comes to setting and reaching goals. That book taught me: 1) The power of believing in possibilities – faith can remove mountains. 2) The people who fail in life are bent on making excuses as to why they can't succeed. 3) Action will cure any fear.

Upon receiving the idea to write this book, I became elated and so absorbed in etching it, so much that one day I decided to pay a visit to the local bookstore. Mainly to see what was on their shelves in the personal development genre for teens. I was sadly disappointed upon discovering that the bookstore carried just a handful of books in that genre for teens, while they displayed hundreds of volumes of the same for adults. I was taken aback. Yes, society has once again failed to score by not realizing this fact: "It is easier to raise a good child than to rehab an adult."

Going back to my roots, I am so grateful for being raised up on strong personal development principles. Values I'd cherish for the rest of my life. Honesty, patience, confidence, faith, enthusiasm, generosity, ambition, appreciation, making a difference passion, purpose and perseverance have in more ways than one, contributed to my value system. Prov. 22:6 states, "Train Children to live the right way, and when they are old, they will not stray from it." This proverb has much to do with the journey called success.

Embarking on my quest, I'm daring you to think outside of the box, act outside of the box, dream outside of the box and the legacy you'll pass on will be one remembered for generations to come. Your grand children and great grand children will never forget your name.

-   JOHN A. ANDREWS

Our deepest fear is not that we are inadequate.
Our deepest fear is that we are powerful beyond measure.
It is our light, not our darkness that most frightens us.

We ask ourselves, who am I to be brilliant, gorgeous, talented
and fabulous?
Actually, who are you not to be?
You are a child of god. Your playing small doesn't serve the
world.

There's nothing enlightened about shrinking so that other people
won't feel insecure around you.
We were born to make manifest the glory of God that is within
us.
It's not just in some of us, it's in everyone.

And, as we let our own light shine, we unconsciously give other
people permission to do the same. As we are liberated from our
own fear, our presence automatically liberates others.[1]

- Marianne Williamson

INTRODUCTION

What do I want to be when I grow up? This is a fundamental question asked by just about every ambitious, visionary teenager and pre-teenager today. They sometimes lock themselves in that world of day dreams and see it unfolding bigger than most of us would – who are already in our prime. You dare not place an obstacle in front of them; they will find a way to remove it. I've watched unnoticed as my sons remove the side bar from their crib in order to escape those four barriers. In a nut shell, they visualized freedom and pursued it. With such a mindset their future always looked bright because they possessed that unstoppable attitude. Consequently their walls tumbled or became penetrable first in their mind before they did in their eyes.

Like the caterpillar going through the cocoon to become a beautiful butterfly, equally, all truly successful people go through walls, which stood in their way towards their destiny. They will also tell you that their success principles were rooted deep inside of them and were the defining agents which helped create the success that you see all around them. If you nurture those roots which run deep within you, your chance of succeeding is inevitable.

Most kids already know who they want to become way before the age of five, and they are not afraid to tell you. To them it's never like a broken record and they repeat it every chance they get. Ask any pre-teen what they want to become when they grow up and they'll confidently respond as that destiny was given to them at birth. You hear it repetitively you'll never ever forget it. With their limited experiences of failure they never surrender to "walls" real or imagined en-route to their accomplishing their desire. They just know that they want it and want it so badly that succeeding seems inevitable. They aren't tentative when it comes to launching out into the unknown.

Making their first step is a classic example. That child would first find an object to support his stance, and then set himself free while maintaining his balance. Suddenly off he goes with that first unsupported step. Even if he falls flat on his face, he gets up and tries again. If he doesn't succeed he tries it again the following day until his mission is accomplished. At such a tender age he understands that if he falls off the horse he must get back on if he's ever going to walk.

I'm always amazed by such genius in kids and their nothing is impossible mindset. However, as these same kids become adults, conditioned by their environment to fail - their goals and dreams suddenly look unreachable. They sometimes let dream stealers question their abilities as well as their ideas. Unintentionally or maliciously (they-use) others inject them with venom, killing their dreams along with their desire to accomplish great things.

Many people, failing to discover themselves go to their grave with their music still unleashed. We mourn their death – a great lose. Conversely we overlook the fact that the greatest **lose** is what died in many of us while we are yet still alive. The King of Pop, Michael Jackson, though experiencing a problematic lifestyle during the years leading up to his death, seemed to be one of the few entertainers of our time who didn't take his music to the grave with him – he certainly *didn't stop til he got enough* and his music was *off the wall*.

I was born in St. Vincent and the Grenadines. And came from a family of eight siblings, although my parents gave birth to eleven, the other two I'd never met. They passed on at an early age. I have five sisters and three brothers and I came in at number eight. Not sure if that number made me the odd ball.

My dad was a carpenter and passed on when I was only nine. Mom was a factory owner. She was confronted with opportunities to remarry during those tough times which followed. Mom turned them all down, stating that her obligations were to the nine of us. She fought through the tough times, not even able to afford me shoes to wear to school. My church shoes were mostly pre-owned and passed down from my elder brother who earned his own wages. I made it a habit of refurbishing them myself. Even if they were too big for my feet I stuffed them with news paper to make them fit. My first new pair of good shoes came a few years before going to high school. They were black leather and fitted comfortably. Before then, my mother bought me a pair of very inexpensive shoes made of rubber – an enemy to the scorching hot sun where I lived.

I was a tough kid bent on doing things my way. The words "John you seem to have a stick broken in your ears" meaning that "*I'm bent on doing things my way no matter what they said*". That statement meant very little to me back then. The phrase, like a broken record was heard constantly from my parents and older siblings alike. So much that I became familiar to the "rod" and they certainly didn't spoil me.

Nevertheless I was tops in my class, got straight A's in just about every subject. I read, and read some more every opportunity I got and studied hard. I made up in activity what I lacked in talent. My small clique of school friends were of the same aptitude though more talented than I was. Running with the ambitious started for me back in my teens and has always remained my mindset and philosophy.

I finished Belmont School at top of my class. I followed that up by excelling in my "(common entrance exams)" the equivalent of the GED exam in the United States. This allowed me to not only enroll at Mountain View Academy, a Christian High School of mom's religion. But, allowed me to skip the first class. My eldest sister was so proud of me she eagerly picked up my tuition for the first two years. A religious school? It was apparent at least what our family envisioned for me. They no doubt saw me probably heading up a church after graduation. They had seen me put benches together, erect a podium and minister to an empty room on numerous occasions.

Mom continued where my sister left off and with some of her meager resources saw me through most of that religious high school. She struggled trying to make ends meet with nine mouths to feed plus hers. I remembered her saying at one point: "John, this is all I can afford." Consequently I dropped out of high school and resorted to learning auto body repairs. If nothing else I did learn a whole lot about discipline and great examples of *faith* from the bible while at the academy. I was so intrigued by the story of Job and his ability to pursue even after he lost all that he had.

My teenage years were molded on strong relationship values – my mom saw to it that they were. She dragged my eight siblings and me to church weekly. She said we had to attend if we lived under her roof. Even if our worship attire had to be recycled, she insisted on our involvement. She talked with other church members about our potential. Mom was very proud of us and of the seeds being sown within us. It didn't matter to her that the weekly two-mile walks each way contributed to wearing out our church shoes. She viewed the process as a by-product of developing fortitude in us.

Mom served as my first personal development coach. Back then she would say, very philosophically: "What you give out in your right hand you're going to receive in your left. You can do whatever you set in your heart and mind to accomplish. If you can think it, you can do it." For a while, I thought she was too immersed in the bible. But some of it did resonate in my delicate mind. One day she told me a story about a woman who went to the river every day, sit down on a huge stone with the soap and laundry next to her, and pray to God that he'd send her help to wash the daily-increasing load. But help never came. She might have had faith, but she wasn't willing to do the work, and help never came.

What are you willing to do with the gifts and abilities you've been endowed with? Is your dare strong enough to cause you to swim upstream when others around you are content to float downstream? The misfits in life are always known to have settled for far less than their best.

I've seen so many "would be greats" who sit on their talent. They have no zest, vim, vitality, passion or sense of purpose. Nothing drives them. They are like a train without a caboose. And they wonder why others are moving ahead in life while they're not. They're waiting for someone to inject them with a dose of success or, like the woman with the laundry, praying that God will bless their idle deeds.

Despite mom's vision for me becoming a pastor, I was obsessed with becoming a police officer when I grew up. So I studied policemen and even prayed to God that someday I would become one. So much that, several of my dreams and nightmares brought the vocation closer to my heart and soul. Would that be my profession? Circumstances changed after coming to America but the deep rooted passion has benefited me tremendously enabling me to write screenplays dealing with law enforcement. There's a famous goal setting quote, "If you shoot for the stars you could end up hitting the trees." How could you miss when you're shooting that high? My peers today know that I'm not only a visionary but much of an enforcer – one who delights in solving problems. I'm thankful that I had such vision and focus as a child, and developed myself in other areas of greatness as well. I like to see myself as an evolving human being, never like a tomato that's ripened but always on the cutting edge.

In 2009 Senator Barack Obama was elected as Americas' first black president. Obama, who rose to great success, grew up during the civil rights revolution of the 1960s, when blacks were not even permitted to ride in the front of the bus as whites did, dine in certain restaurants or even permitted to vote. In those days "segregation" was not only an academic institutional slogan, but rather an uncomfortable household word to the negro race. Bottom line: back then severe limits were placed on the associations of these two races - with blacks at a stringent disadvantage. Obama went through those walls and consequently earned the American vote.

During that civil rights era of intense racial conflicts, leaders such as Malcolm X and Dr. Martin Luther King Jr. emerged on the scene. King, a black man from the south fought for, and lost his life (assassinated) daring to fulfill his dream of equality. A dream that:

> *One day his children would not be judged by the color of their skin but by the content of their character.*[2] In addition: *that one day all children regardless of the color of their skin would live together in unity.*[3]

In 1969 a school teacher by day and an insurance agent by night from Oklahoma City, Harland Stonecipher, was involved in a head on collision automobile accident. His car got totaled as a result. The police officer called to the scene cited the other driver, a woman, at fault who then turned around and sued Harland Stonecipher. He was not only hospitalized but he exhausted his life savings of almost $4,000.00 defending himself against that lawsuit. He ended up winning but felt as though he had lost. In today's economy that sum would equal almost $40,000.00.

Consequently, Harland searched not only the U.S but also Europe and found out that most Europeans owned a legal plan in order to protect their rights. He adopted the concept and brought it to America, and now almost two million families have access to top quality advice whenever they need it for just over a dollar a day. Because of this adversity his destiny now embodies a two-fold mission. (1) To provide equal justice under law for all North American families. (2)To create more millionaires than any other company has ever created in history.[3]

Oprah Winfrey, although born in poverty and a victim of abuse and a troubled youth, rose to become by far the most powerful woman of our time. Oprah spent the kindergarten stage of her life living with her grandmother, who provided her with a strong disciplinary environment in which the church played a vital role.

One day Oprah stunned church members by delivering a reading and interpretation of a passage from the bible. Her grandmother taught her how to read and those skills were later honed by her grandfather. She was required to read books and, every two weeks, to write a report about what she had read. Oprah would often say that she wanted to make her living by talking. It was said that she became a gifted and quick-witted speaker. She knew way back then what she wanted to become, even though she grew up during the civil rights revolution when segregation was prevalent.

In 1972 she became the first black woman to hold the anchor position at Nashville's WTVF-TV. In 1986 she launched the Oprah Winfrey Show. In 1994 she bought her own studio "Harpo." In 1996 she began Oprah's book club to promote reading, for which she recommends a recently published book each month. She sets aside one show each month for a full discussion on the book. She has since created her classic book club which features 3 authors per year. Oprah habitually gives 10% of her income to charities, mostly having to do with youths, education and books.[4]

Oprah Winfrey, who became a billionaire at age 49, has not only risen to become the most powerful and influential woman in television but ruler of a large entertainment and communications empire - from a life of poverty and abuse to one of greatness. Oprah at one point in her broadcast career believed in herself so much, sources close to her knew that she was like a hit record to be released. It wasn't long before she became that hit record. She has broken down so many walls. Now when she talks - people absolutely listen.

Pastors Philip and Holly Wagner reside in Los Angeles, California. I first met them in 2001 at the Oasis Christian Center. Holly is a former actress and Philip, a pastor's kid came from a home of devout Baptists. Born in the sixties Philip could not escape racial injustice seen firsthand by his parents. Together they started the church at a home bible study in Beverly Hills, California with 10 people in attendance. This grew to about 60 people, and then declined from week to week. In those early years they would tell you that they struggled with their relationship. After 24 years this church, situated in the heart of Hollywood now resembles the United Nations because of its many diverse ethnicities in attendance and has now grown to over 2,000 members strong. Today the church not only quenches the spiritual thirst of many Southern Californians but supports several mission outreach programs around the world.

Philip was very instrumental in the creation of "Generosity Water" an organization which gives 100% of its profits towards building water wells in Uganda and other countries. That organization has now built over 50 water wells for Ugandan residents.[5]

In fulfilling their destiny, Philip and Holly have not only removed the walls of racism and social injustice but have also taught many seminars on relationships around the world while constantly working on theirs.

Is your destiny one of greatness – a cause greater than self? There are things you and I will accomplish in our lifetime that will not only astonish our relatives, friends, neighbors, co-workers but our enemies alike. It has been discovered that 90% of an iceberg rests beneath the surface. It may surprise you that each of us has at least 90% of our potential lying untapped. As human beings we are known to only use that other 10% of our potential.

In my interaction with successful people from all walks of life, I've discovered that they are not only specialists in their field but that they had at one point in their lives said **yes** to their potential. In my journey up the ladder of success, I've learned to become as "a sponge" by learning from them. I've worn their shoes, and felt some of their pain. You will meet most of them through these pages as you will me. Most of all because success leaves clues, you will discover that they recognized their value, believed in their value, increased their value, and consequently they've become valuable.

Our world has been searching for you. It needs people who are willing to step off the sidelines and into the game - willing to make a significant difference.

"I DARE YOU TO ACHIEVE SOMETHING THAT WILL MAKE THE FUTURE POINT TO YOU WITH EVEN MORE PRIDE THAN THE PRESENT IS POINTING TO THOSE WHO HAVE GONE BEFORE YOU."

- WILLIAM DANFORTH

Chapter One

POTENTIAL

In his book, *The Genius Machine,* author Gerald Sindell asks: "How can you get out of your own ocean to see what differentiates you?"[2] Based on the worlds populous of almost seven billion people, **you** stand out. You might reason – Really? Me? No Way! That's impossible. I am nobody. I don't have the brains. I am from the wrong side of the tracks. I don't have what it takes I am not the best tool in the shed. I am not, I am not, and I am not. If you are holding onto those false beliefs about yourself – Understand, they are nothing but figments of your imagination.

Think about the last time you were looking at a collection of pictures. Did you find yourself looking for you, even when you knew you weren't in the picture? It's our human tendency to look first to see if we are included because it's all about what's in it for me or where do I fit into the scheme of things. Also, if you were to, with time permitting, check out the entire world's population, you won't find anyone exactly like you, including anyone with your particular abilities, intelligence or viewpoint. Have you ever pondered and come to the realization that there's a reason why you are the only one with your voice, thumb print along with many other attributes?

What if I was to tell you that you have the power within you to become successful? That you have the in this moment, a power which lays dormant, like a volcano. When discovered and tapped into, will erupt and lift you from failure to success. This power can assist you in transforming into a person who can experience tremendous influence and success. I know this may be hard to believe, comprehend or figure out. What I were to tell you is that all you have to do is to trust **your** power by *knowing yourself*? In his book **On Becoming a Leader** Warren Bennis writes,

> *"Know thyself, then, means separating who you are and who you want to be from what the world thinks you are and wants you to be."*[2]

It is often said that KNOWLEDGE IS POWER. Self knowledge is your first key to success. What I really want you to know is that if you really, I MEAN REALLY, REALLY know yourself, you'd understand that the sky is the limit to your potential! Knowing that alone would keep you up at night, unable to go to sleep, so excited about what can be! You'd be so captivated by such a burning desire to tap into and unleash your 90% unused potential. You'd be wide awake, planning the next series of moves for your life.

What are you willing to do to live your full potential?

 ➢ Are you willing to believe in yourself.

 ➢ Are you willing to incorporate new habits.

 ➢ Are you willing to associate with those who have your best in mind.

 ➢ Are you willing to develop a sense of passion. and purpose towards fulfilling your destiny?

 ➢ Would you, in exchange for a better, fuller and richer life step up to the plate?

YOU must realize that you're different. You are unique. You are beauty-fully and wonder-fully made. You are here, right now, and no one can be you but you. Be excitingly thankful and appreciative for who you are as well as who you can become. That's the power of tapping your potential.

Unfortunately and tragically, as human beings we place very little value on ourselves and subsequently acclimatize toward failure. We live in a world bombarded with negative news, pessimism and a mediocrity mindset. As a result, devaluing ourselves has become such an easy thing to do. Watching constant negative news for a few hours over a period of time and we are hooked, immersed in all that negativity. As the saying goes, "Garbage in garbage out." We hear and watch so much violence, now we're even afraid to go outside. Not only that, we've not only become fearful of others but also we fear our own potential resulting in living our life hiding our light from not only ourselves, but the world. The following is one of my favorite readings by Marianne Williamson:

> *Our deepest fear is not that we are inadequate.*
> *Our deepest fear is that we are powerful beyond measure.*
> *It is our light, not our darkness that most frightens us.*
>
> *We ask ourselves, who am I to be brilliant, gorgeous, talented and fabulous?*
> *Actually, who are you not to be?*
> *You are a child of god. Your playing small doesn't serve the world.*
>
> *There's nothing enlightened about shrinking so that other people won't feel insecure around you.*
> *We were born to make manifest the glory of God that is within us.*
> *It's not just in some of us, it's in everyone.*
>
> *And, as we let our own light shine, we unconsciously give other people permission to do the*

same. As we are liberated from our own fear, our presence automatically liberates others.[1]

Growing up as I kid I was always laughed at, called names such as ugly and skinny. None of those fit with who I am today. As a result, my self image was negatively impacted. Even if my mom instilled positive reinforcement, because my association with my classmates lasted much longer than the time I'd spent with her - I became negatively affected.

As an adult I've had to read many books on personal development in order to dilute those toxins and rediscover who I really am and could become. Today those names have become nothing but water under a bridge because I've constantly and consistently worked on myself.

As a responsible teenager on your way to the top, realize that you are always looking at two different walls. You'll find that one says you are top notch and you can do whatever you can think, want or desire. You have all the resources and support to make things happen. You were born to succeed. Nothing can stop you. Everything you touch turns to gold. Your unlimited potential will propel you to the top in your chosen vocation. You are enough.

The other wall says: You grew up on the wrong side of the tracks, you can't do anything right, You will never have what you want. You have no capital or other resources and no one believes in you. You never follow through and finish things. You fail at everything you do. You don't have the right education and training. You are TOO--- EVERYTHING!

Conversely, when it comes down to making a difference, everything starts with you. Once you really launch out, you'll discover if bent on success that:

> You are in the driver's seat.
> You call the shots.
> You are the captain of your own ship.
> You are the pilot of your own aircraft.
> You set your own pace.

Most of all, you are the only wall you must encounter towards your destiny. You chose success or failure. The ball is in your hands – you dribble or you shoot.

An individual focused on success must eliminate the blame game completely from one's mindset in order to have *true* success. If indulged, it becomes obvious that when pointing a finger at someone else, *there are three pointing back at them*. Instead, whenever the chips are down, they "saddle up" and focus on their destiny. In doing so one develops the morale that "It's all or nothing." He/She eats, breathes and lives success creating war on any "habit" which has kept or will keep one captive. With such a mindset in place, stepping out of one's comfort zone becomes an embracing challenge. Consequently, this move most likely results in a much richer and rewarding lifestyle. In my book *When the Dust Settles* I refer to the story about the baby elephant chained to a stake, and after several years, later, with the chain removed from its feet, the elephant refused from setting itself free. It didn't know what or how to be due to its longtime conditioning. To the elephant, the chain was still there.

How are you *chained* to you circumstances?

Living such a life chained to your circumstances is a chain you must break if your advancing is going to be inevitable.

Breaking yourself free and being all you can be will take some effort on your part. Similarly success is a choice, path taken purposefully and filled with both challenges and learning opportunities. I'm always reminded of the story of two men waiting at the dock.

> One man looked like he had been waiting there forever, putrid and unkept. A ship pulled up,

dropped anchor and the agile man, while boarding said, "Good to see you again, pal." Then he jumped aboard the ship. Before setting sail he asked the waiting man: "What are you waiting for pal? I see you here all the time..." The waiting man responded: "My ship, of course." The man on the moving ship retorted, "Did you send one out? "No" the unkept man replied. "Sorry, you have to send one out and in some cases swim out to meet it."

So many people are waiting for their ship to come in when they've never sent one out. They anticipate receiving without first giving, reaping without sowing. They are always looking for that someone to hand them something.

A film producer friend of mine, produced a film in 2004, and has experienced the thrill of that growing movie franchise, generating over $100,000,000 from the last 5 yearly installments. To a person with a failure mindset, it looks like he was lucky, and to those who are success minded they know that it took more than luck. I've known him over ten years and consider him as someone with tremendous work ethics. Before his big break five years ago I'd seen him reading screenplay after screenplay and novel after novel looking for the right one to turn into a movie.

Noticing his passionate appetite I handed him scripts that I thought would be of interest.

One day before his big break my sons and I paid him a visit. He asked if we could watch his son play in the backyard while he caught up on his script reading, I obliged. As an actor in a movie which he produced starring actor *Denzel Washington,* I saw him engrossed in a novel during the lunch break. An acquaintance of mine also told me that one day he saw him on an airplane with over six scripts in his briefcase. Today he is one of the top independent producers in Hollywood living a phenomenal lifestyle, one to be greatly desired. This is one example of a person's commitment to doing what was necessary in order to live their passion and dream. In this case, he was always reading scripts, looking for the best and right one. As you can see, he sent out many ships and they returned!

In reading this *Success 101,* you will find that in order to excel you've got to commit to growing up, and taking on the responsibilities of life. Therefore, working on one's self takes precedence.

In order to become a beautiful butterfly the caterpillar needs to first go inward and spin a cocoon. The cocoon allows it to grow and develop, focused only on these two things so it can become a beautiful butterfly. By doing so, when it emerges, it now is able to fly from flower to flower pollinating them in the process. Becoming successful is much like becoming a butterfly. It asks you to develop and focus your potential.

Each of us has talents and abilities lying dormant in us mainly because we don't have the courage to dig them up and put them to use. Many times during conversations, people who know me as an author often mention that they want to write a book or have started writing a book but have never finished it. I normally respond with, "If you really want to do it, tonight before you go to bed embark on the process of creating the outline or dust off the computer's keyboard and continue writing." How many of them do it? I can tell not many – only the ones who dare.

In his book *I Dare You* author William Danforth writes:

"I dare you to achieve something that will make the future point to you with even more pride than the present is pointing to those who have gone before you."[1]

Success is a journey. Though many think it's a destination. The people who continue to succeed value themselves and who are constantly working on changing and enhancing their self image. They feel as though they have not yet "scratched the scratch" in their chosen endeavor. They realize that success is all about taking action and dares anyone to outwork them. In essence their life has to be a worthwhile endeavor. The championship, the super bowl, the bestseller, the Oscar, the crowd's approval, the gold medal, the one million church members in attendance, and receiving of the Nobel Prize are all great accomplishments, yet those high achievers are not at all satisfied. They see the world as if it's a complex jig saw puzzle and they are the only missing piece towards the solution. They think "If it's going to be, it's up to me."

It doesn't matter who you are, where you are, where you live, what you have or don't have, who are your parents, or how low your grades are right now. **You have got potential!**

If you dare to make a difference, you have enlisted yourself in a great cause that will certainly bless humanity beyond your imagination. Mahatma Gandhi once said:

"Be the change you wish to see in the world."[4]

YOU no doubt by reading this book have already defined yourself as a person who wants more for their life. If you are not in pursuit of your own success, feel free to pass this volume on to someone else desiring all they have ever wanted to become. However, if you have a burning desire to go through those walls standing in your way AND if you care enough to succeed massively, AND are willing to tap into your potential - your SUCCESS is inevitable!

With every journey it takes commitment. Oftentimes, I have seen teens loaded with potential who fail to step up. Fear of commitment is one of the main causes of the lazy person's disease known as "fence sitting." Lack of commitment in any endeavor could be attributed to the inability to tie into the vision. Resulting in an, unfulfilled dream.

When one embraces a vision, like the employees did back at NASA before the first attempt to put a man on the moon, then momentum emerges, and the organization or individual becomes unstoppable. There always seems to be something extra that radiates from someone once they commit.

In life we find, that when we are interested in something we tend to do it when it is convenient. When we are committed, we do it no matter what stands in our way – regardless of the crisis.

Have you ever met people who delight in sitting on

their "good intentions?" They boast, "I have a cause, I have been thinking about it since I was five years old. Someday I'll make it happen. When it gets launched, it will totally save the world." It is the best thing since "sliced bread." Unfortunately, they never do anything about it.

Total commitment to your desires allows you to move toward your world, enabling your world to move towards you. When you *launch* out, you create waves, and only by doing so can you attract committed energy into your sail.

What do you dare to achieve using your full potential?

"IF AN ORGANIZATION DOESN'T HAVE A CLEAR PURPOSE AND SENSE OF WHAT BUSINESS IT'S IN, WE THINK THERE'S SOMETHING WRONG. YET FEW PEOPLE HAVE A CLEAR SENSE OF THEIR LIFE'S PURPOSE. HOW CAN YOU MAKE GOOD DECISIONS ABOUT HOW YOU SHOULD USE YOUR TIME IF YOU DON'T KNOW WHAT BUSINESS YOU'RE IN?"

- KEN BLANCHARD.

Chapter Two

PURPOSE

In the *The Purpose Driven Life*, Rick Warren writes: "Living on purpose is the only way to really live. Everything else is just existing."[2] Too many of us drift along with the wrong crowd going nowhere fast. In *The Master Key To Riches* author napoleon Hill recounts a statement by Andrew Carnegie, the man who developed a fortune by going the extra mile:

> *"The person who is motivated by definiteness of purpose and moves on that purpose with the spiritual forces of his being may challenge those who are indecisive at the post and pass them at the grandstand. It makes no difference whether someone is selling life insurance or digging ditches."*[3]

It's a known fact that physically and mentally lazy people tend to remain in their comfort zone far too long. At that desolate place no more growth ever occurs. Consequently, they never fully realize the good they often might win by stepping off the sidelines and into the game. Subsequently, their purpose remains undefined, unsupported and un-realized. They fail miserably in that effort to grow, stretch and become all they can be.

We live in a world full of half-alive people who no longer believe in themselves. Alive at age 35 but mentally most are already dead and buried. The good life eludes them. Any professional bodybuilder would tell you that a muscle only grows when it's stretched. The sleeping giants within you need to be activated. James Allen states in *As a Man Thinketh*:

> *Those who have no central purpose in life fall an easy prey to petty worries, fears, troubles and self pitying, all of which are indications of weakness, which lead just as surely as deliberately planned sins (though by a different route) to failure, unhappiness, and loss. For weakness cannot persist in a power-evolving universe. We should conceive of a legitimate purpose in our hearts and set out to accomplish it.*[4]

There's a war to be fought. **Yours!** Yes, lifting your head up above the crowd will give you purpose, ammunition and direction in life. You will see where you need to go. And the world always seems to make way for the person who knows where he or she is going. Streets are crowded; a fire engine is coming through. Everything gives way; pedestrians, vehicles, everything. They all step aside for this speeding machine on a mission. Why? It has a purpose – putting out the fire and it has a sense of urgency in doing so.

THE CHAMPION

The average runner sprints
Until the breath in him is gone
But the champion has the iron will
That makes him "carry on.

For rest, the average runner begs
When limp his muscles grow
But the champion runs on leaden legs
His spirit makes him go.

The average man's complacent
When he does his best to score
But the champion does his best
And then he does a little more.

- Author unknown.

A purpose driven individual will readily discover within that "extra-ness" necessary to overcoming all odds. The words "I can't" are totally eliminated from his or her vocabulary. Whenever he's confronted with any sign of defeat he resolves: "I am not giving up, bring it on. It might lick some, but not me. I absolutely will not be denied!" Author Julia Cameron writing in her book *The Artist's Way* says,

> *"I have learned, as a rule of thumb, never to ask whether you can do something. Say, instead, that you are doing it. Then fasten your seat belt. The most remarkable thing follows."*[5] Additionally she states, *"Take a small step in the direction of a dream and watch the synchronous doors flying open."* **A maxim worth remembering**, *"Leap, and the net will appear."*[6]

That door, one day opened for director Steven Spielberg. He visualized making a unique film. With the script already in possession he needed a producer to finance it. One day while he was walking on the beach he encountered a man who not only had the resources but was willing to invest in young film makers. This total stranger stepped up to the plate and gave Spielberg the money, enabling him to shoot *Amblin.* That film was given an honorable mention at the Venice Film Festival and opened the door for him coming to Hollywood. The rest is history.[7]

When we know what we want and embark upon accomplishing it, amazing things occur. Let's visit with some purpose driven individuals who no doubt will take away the excuses of many.

Human Activist, Helen Keller could have said "Me? I was born blind and deaf."

Inventor, Thomas A Edison could have said "Who needs an incandescent light bulb? I have already tried 10,999 times."

Steve Jobs, the founder of Apple computers, could have said "I'm way too young to achieve massive success." He made his first million at age twenty-three, his first ten million at twenty-four, and at age twenty-five his first 100 million.

President Abraham Lincoln could have said "I am a big failure politically. I have already lost eighteen elections. I would never become the American president."

President, Nelson Mandela could have said "My own country men threw me in jail, where I've spent most of my life. I could never become the president of my country."

Colonel Sanders, the founder of Kentucky Fried Chicken could have said "I dropped out of high school plus I 'm way over 40 - way too old to succeed in life." He didn't fulfill his dream until age 65 and received 1,009 "NO'S" before he got a "YES."[8]

Paul Getty, the world's first billionaire could have said "I'm not born a businessman. I have no business being in business." Yet he became a model for some of the most successful business people of our time. Getty said,

> "I'd rather have 1 % of the efforts of a hundred men than 100% of my own efforts."[9]

He owns the Getty Museum in Los Angeles, California. One of my associates, about this huge landmark remarks: "Getty owns a mountain and that's the only man I know to do so."

President, John F. Kennedy could have said "I am too young to become the American president; no one is going to listen to me."

President, Truman could have said "I have never been to college I could never become president of America."

Artists, Ray Charles and Stevie Wonder could have said "We are blind, how are we going to find the keys to the piano, much less sing to an audience who we cannot see."

Charlie Chaplin, one of history's wealthiest actors could have said "I grew up in poverty roaming the streets of London. I'll never amass a fortune."

Astronaut, Neil Armstrong could have said 'The moon is so out of reach, I have no business going up there."

Most people lack the initiative needed in order to become all they were meant to be, mainly because they don't believe deep down inside that they are valuable. Therefore they live a purpose deprived life.

> Purpose, a *directive* word, which means heading towards something, gains momentum when meshed with the *propellant* word belief – that feeling knowing that you can do whatever you set out to do. People, lacking the propellant in their own mindset and philosophy usually look for this additive coming from someone else's, and when they don't receive it, they wonder why their life spins around like a top in mud – going nowhere fast. In order to take advantage of others believing in you, you must first harness the power of belief in yourself.

When a commercial airplane is getting ready for takeoff, first the doors are closed shut. Passenger's seat belts are securely fastened. The plane then taxis down the runway in preparation for takeoff. The air traffic controllers in the control tower are aware that the plane is ready for takeoff. Instruction is then given to the pilot to speed up. He releases the throttle, retracts the landing gear and engages the skies.

Believing in yourself will initiate purpose. **Belief: that ability necessary to taxi down the runway in your preparation for takeoff.** As soon as others start believing in you, your ascent becomes eminent. *All things are possible to him who believes.* Successful people believed that they were going to be successful and set sail in pursuit of their objective. Their lives became driven by that burning desire to succeed. They knew where they were going and consequently found their hidden guides to take them there. It is often said "When the student is ready the teacher appears."

As an immigrant to the United States several years ago, I sensed that Americans are so fortunate because of the many opportunities which exist in this country, and that they often take their heritage for granted.

Conversely, back then I felt like the odds were stacked against me, coming from the Caribbean and not being able to master the Standard American English. I still speak with an island flavor. Nevertheless, I learned to grasp those opportunities which could lead me to the next level.

Consequently, some amazing people have stepped into my life as guides, including my mentor and friend Bob Wilson. He had just retired after teaching elementary and high school teacher for a period of 35 years. We first met when he played my Dad in a student film - the adaptation of *Guess Who Is Coming To Dinner*. This was my first film project when I moved to Hollywood in 1996. He has always guided me back on the right path, especially during those early years of my divorce, and has played the role of a devil's advocate on numerous occasions. Additionally, Bob has helped me to validate my belief in myself, as I dare to make a difference.

Belief in self is paramount if there is ever going to be any worthwhile accomplishment. Remember, no one else really believes in you until you first believe in yourself.

> *If an organization doesn't have a clear purpose and sense of what business it's in, we think there's something wrong. Yet few people have a clear sense of their life's purpose. How can you make good decisions about how you should use your time if you don't know what business you're in?*[1] Ken Blanchard, **Leading At A Higher Level.**

Once you are airborne, and the fasten-your-seatbelt sign is off, you are now not only committed to fly to your destination with a purpose in mind, but at what speed.

What do you think is your purpose in life.

"DEVELOP A PASSION FOR LEARNING. IF YOU DO, YOU WILL NEVER CEASE TO GROW."

-ANTHONY J. D'ANGELO

Chapter Three

PASSION

You have already tapped into your potential, you understand your purpose, but how driven are you towards becoming the person you were really meant to be? Some people live their lives in a lukewarm "whatever happens" state. Water is known to boil at 211 degrees and at 212 degrees turn to steam enough to push any locomotive. That extra one degree has propelled many from failure to amazing success.

Do you have the zeal to make things happen? When you feel that zest, excitement, focus and burning desire to accomplish something: that's passion running through your being. Without your passion, no one will see your potential. There's plenty of room at the top but not too many are passionate enough about getting there. That's why they never arrive. They act as if they have forever to live and unfortunately the successful-good-life eludes them.

Everything that exists was first an idea acted upon either by you or someone else. As a writer I've met so many people with an idea for the next bestseller or the next hit movie and yet they never write it.

Consequently their idea never makes it to the book shelf or the screen. What would happen if you were told that you only have ONE month to live? How zealous would you be about getting things done? Would that back burner where "dreams that can wait" are stored be full or empty? What would be your commitment level, 10, 90 or 150?

Some people like to watch things happen, some people like to wonder what will happen, and some people don't really care what happens. But the action-driven person delights in making things happen. Become branded for doing things. When you see something that ought to be done, step up to the plate and hit the home run. Once you acquire the action habit, others have no choice but to step aside for you. Take one step forward in the direction of your goals and dreams and your adversaries will run for cover. They see your obvious passion and determination.

In *The 5 Steps To Changing Your Life* I also related a story about a young man who was working as a second hand on a railroad. His thoroughness sub-sequently won him an opportunity to work in a shipping office. During the interim the substitute clerk asked this young man for some facts and figures. The young man didn't know anything about bookkeeping, but he spent three days and three nights without sleep and had the facts ready for the superintendent when he returned. That passionate act of decision and commitment later propelled him into the vice-presidency seat of his own company.

Successful people make it a habit of getting things done while unsuccessful people are habitual procrastinators. A successful person sees a great opportunity such as to go into business for himself while the unsuccessful person doesn't take action and that trend passes him by. He subsequently misses out on the opportunity to become a profiteer and resorts himself to the status of a consumer.

The great opportunities in life are captured by those who take action, not by those who wait. "The early bird catches the worm" while the late bird removes the dirt in hope of finding worms.

Let's visit with a passionate driven individual, Bill Gates, who did what it took to make his goals and dreams come true. Notice he didn't let things get in the way.

In 1975 Bill Gates dropped out of Harvard to pursue his career as a software designer. He later was joined by his colleague Paul Allen in the co-founding venture of Microsoft. It was rumored that Gates also showed the concept to two of his other colleagues who said no. Other sources claimed that Gates had a cot in his office that he slept on night after night for several years when he was getting Microsoft off the ground. In 1980 Gates developed the Microsoft Disk Operating System (MS-DOS). And he successfully sold IBM on this new operating system.

By the 1990s Microsoft had sold more than 100 million copies of MS-DOS making the operating system the all-time leader in software sales.

Gates' competitive drive and fierce desire to win has made him a powerful force in business. It was his passion for his product and what it would do for the world that kept him committed to endure setbacks, such as lawsuits he encountered along the way. It also consumed much of his personal life. In the six years between 1978 and 1984, he took a total of only two weeks vacation. On New Year's Day 1994 Gates married Melinda French, a Microsoft manager, on the Hawaiian island of Lanai. His fortune at the time of his marriage was estimated at close to seven billion dollars. By 1997 his worth was estimated at approximately $37 billion, earning him the title of "Richest man in America."

His contributions really amaze me.

> *Aside from being the most famous businessman of the late 1990s, Gates also has distinguished himself as a philanthropist. He and wife Melinda established the Bill & Melinda Gates Foundation, which focuses on helping to improve health care and education for children around the world. The foundation has donated $4 billion since its start in 1996. Recent pledges include $1 billion over twenty years to fund college scholarships for about one thousand minority students; $750 million over five years to help launch the Global Fund for Children's Vaccines; $50 million to help the World Health Organization's efforts to eradicate polio, a crippling disease that usually attacks children; and $3 million to help prevent the spread of acquired immune deficiency syndrome (AIDS; an incurable disease that destroys the body's immune system) among young people in South Africa. In November 1998 Gates and his wife also gave the largest single gift to a U.S. public library, when they donated $20 million to the Seattle Public Library. Another of Gates' charitable donations was $20 million given to the Massachusetts Institute of Technology to build a new home for its Laboratory for Computer Science.*

In July 2000 the foundation gave John Hopkins University a five-year, $20 million grant to study whether or not inexpensive vitamin and mineral pills can help save lives in poor countries. On November 13, 2000, Harvard University's School of Public Health announced it had received $25 million from the foundation to study AIDS prevention in Nigeria. The grant was the largest single private grant in the school's history. It was announced on February 1, 2001, that the foundation would donate $20 million to speed up the global eradication (to completely erase) of the disease commonly known as elephantiasis, a disease that causes disfigurement. In 2002 Gates, along with rock singer Bono, announced plans for DATA Agenda, a $24 billion fund (partially supported by the Bill and Melinda Gates Foundation) that seeks to improve health care in Africa.[3]

Although Gates' parents had a law career in mind for their son, he developed his early interest for computers which turned into his passion, resulting in the Microsoft phenomenon. Additionally, Gates attributes his success to reading the biographies of successful people over a long period of time. His philanthropic life-style and contribution to technology continues to make a difference.

Let's visit with another passion driven individual,

Rosa Parks, a lady with no excuses in her way.

One December evening in 1955, a seamstress for a department store in Montgomery, Alabama boarded a city bus en-route to her home. It was during the civil rights revolution, when blacks were only legally permitted to sit at the back of a bus. She walked passed the "whites only" section towards the middle of the bus.

With frequent stops the bus filled up. The driver, a white man, noticed that more people of his race were still boarding. So he ordered the people in the seamstress Rosa Parks' row to move to the back of the bus. Apparently they gave him a deaf ear. Frustrated, he barked at those black passengers, they all got up except for Rosa Parks.

Consequently she was arrested and sent to jail after a sheriff was called to the scene.[4] Parks' passionate act fueled the already simmering civil rights movement with Martin Luther King at the helm. Today in America, not only are blacks and other minorities permitted to vote but we now have a black man now sitting in the White House as our Commander and Chief.

Which situation could you change for the better if you are passionate about making a difference in the world?

In 2002 I made several phone calls for at least three weeks to find out who held the rights to a 1970s classic film which I so passionately wanted to remake. When I located the studio I called them to enquire about acquiring the rights to the film. A woman answered the phone and I was informed that, "sorry, we don't give up those rights to any third party." That ticked me off as I was so bent on remaking that movie.

Without hesitation I called a writer friend who had his script already optioned with a major studio and asked if he'd be willing to help me write my pet project. See, after being denied those rights, I decided that I was going to write my own screenplay and someday they will come begging for it. My friend told me that because he was signed with a manager it would be impossible for him to collaborate writing a script with me. He did however; sent me templates for writing a screenplay.

At the time, I didn't know how to use a computer's keyboard accurately. I had never taken a typing class. Nonetheless, I embarked upon writing my script using my right hand calculating the use of each key while looking to see what was written on the screen. I was passionate about wanting to write and did. I became unstoppable!

Later I showed one of my screenplays to a director I knew. He responded with an email stating that it was the worse screenplay he'd ever read and that I should give it up. As if that wasn't enough he stated that I was a novice. I didn't write anything for over a week and later returned to the drawing board; writing as if I was a maniac. About a year later I purposely sent him one of my scripts. A few days later my phone rang, it was him. "John how are you, mate?" "AWSOME" I replied. "Great work! Not too many people know how to write action thrillers. It's a tough genre. You have got the knack."

"Thanks" I replied even more enthusiastically. I was stoked, as my passion and determination was starting to pay off.

With a few screenplays already written and more in the works including my upcoming Hollywood Story, I'm very passionate about what lies ahead. In the words of Anthony J. D'Angelo,

"Develop a passion for learning. If you do, you will never cease to grow."[1]

My typing style has not changed much since my writing debut. I refused from letting that temporary handicap fence me in with my vision sitting on the launching pad. I've decided to become unstoppable.

I believe in a source greater than me and knowing that if the thought occurs, it can be written.

"WHEN PEOPLE FEEL GOOD ABOUT YOU AND THEMSELVES DURING THE TIMES THEY'RE WITH YOU, THEN YOUR LEVEL OF INFLUENCE INCREASES SIGNIFICANTLY."

- JOHN MAXWELL

Chapter Four

PERSONALITY

Successful people always seem to exude that indescribable quality which attracts you to them like freckles of steel to magnet. You feel it in their handshake, their pat on the back. You hear it in their intonations, their looking you in the eye, and in their charismatic smile. They totally have "IT" and it's called personality. They draw you in. Indescribable, yet it moves you.

- ➤ Where does personality come from?
- ➤ Is it something we are born with?
- ➤ Can it be developed?
- ➤ How do we get it?

It can be acquired if you are willing to work on yourself.

Benjamin Franklin began as a printer's apprentice and later became the first self made millionaire in America. He adapted a process of personal development strategies. As a young man he struggled realizing that he was somewhat ill mannered and argumentative, character traits which he realized was creating animosity toward him from his co-workers and associates as well. In an effort to change he rewrote the script of his personality. Franklin began by making a list of what that ideal person should possess.

Franklin then concentrated on developing one virtue each week. Some of those thirteen virtues included: tranquility, moderation, resolution, humility, order and temperance. He practiced and worked hard at these virtues. As a routine he would practice one virtue each week, then two weeks, then three weeks, then for a one month period until it became a part of his character.

As a result he not only became one of the most popular personalities but also very influential as well. His influence played a very important role as an ambassador from the United States during the constitutional convention, when the constitution and the Bill of Rights for the United States was debated, negotiated and agreed upon.[2] By daring to work on himself he made himself into a person capable of shaping the course of history.

Some people have a greater capacity for developing personality traits more than others. And this has a lot to do with their social upbringing. A child who is raised in a home where there is "high and high standards," is more likely to develop these personality traits. However, many others overcome adversity and chose to develop these personality traits moving in the direction of success.

The people who've learned from their failures like Benjamin Franklin have been knocked down so many times that they not only embrace "getting back up" with a smile but embraced the adversity simultaneously, knowing that they will get back up and you better watch out when they do. Successful people tend to turn "IT" on like magic. Their magnetism wins you and draws you in wanting to know more about them.

I've always made it a habit to learn something from the personality of every successful person I've encountered. Most of all I've noticed and admired this special trait, which is a characteristic of great leadership - the ability to solve problems. Obstacles have no chance, at least not for long. They have that leaders' mindset.

When I first met Mr. Stonecipher he greeted me with a firm handshake, and he conveyed in his "good to meet you" the message that "John the world needs you." That interaction spoke directly to my potential. That exchange gave such a tremendous boast to my self-esteem. How can I ever forget about my destiny whenever I associate with personalities like him?

Have you ever seen someone enter a room and immediately – charismatically – attract the warmth and attention of others? Understand, they were not born this way. One thing is for sure, they have become this way as a result of their many trials and failures as well as successes along the way. They have learned how to laugh at the adversities life brings their way. Personalities who have made success their vocation are like that whether you meet them on the top of a mountain or down in a valley. In good times or bad, they have the knack for attracting people.

These twelve traits speak volume about an individual with an attractive personality.

1. He has conquered selfishness, others have become his priority.
2. He knows that he'll reap what he sows. Therefore he sows his best.
3. He exercises self control.
4. He listens to others.
5. He gives with no strings attached.
6. He recognizes value in others.

7. He appreciates what others intend, not only what they do.
8. He lifts others up.
9. He's positive about life.
10. He leads and inspires others. When people leave his presence they feel better about themselves.
11. He is a servant leader.
12. He keeps increasing his own value.

His leadership has influence. He lifts you to higher ground. Brian Tracy, in his book *Million Dollar Habits* writes:

> *Make it a habit to go through life doing and saying the things that raise the self-esteem of others and make them feel valuable.*[3]

In his book *Becoming a Person of Influence* John Maxwell writes:

> *When people feel good about you and themselves during the times they're with you, then your level of influence increases significantly.*[1]

By now I hope you have a new outlook on life with a new feeling about yourself. By adopting the personality traits outlined in this chapter, you would discover it is easiest for you to meet the needs of others once your needs has been met. You would become a people magnet attracting others who will support you getting towards the next level and your destiny. Consequently, a domino effect is created causing others to win because you've won.

How do you measure up to the 12 traits?

"YOU WILL NEVER MAKE IT UPSTREAM WITH ONLY A MERE WISH. THE RAPIDS ARE FIERCE; THEY'LL PUSH YOU BACK DOWNSTREAM TOWARD SELF PITY AND MEDIOCRITY IF YOUR RESOLVE ISN'T STRONG ENOUGH."

-JOHN A. ANDREWS

Chapter Five

VISION

"Where there is no vision the people perish." This philosophy and mindset works without fail every time and is applicable to every area of a person's life. John F. Kennedy the youngest American president said this:

> *"The problems of the world cannot possibly be solved by skeptics or cynics whose horizons are limited by obvious realities. We need men who can dream of things that never were."*[1]

No one succeeds without a vision. Let me explain - I am not talking about acquiring success without paying the full price. Like someone who wins the lottery for example. You may say what about receiving an inheritance? Isn't that luck? An inheritance (money and other personal things) is a good thing to leave behind. I believe that every successful person should leave a legacy, leaving something that cannot be shaken and here for future generations For example: Reggae artist, the late Bob Marley's *name* will never be forgotten because of his legendary contribution to music. And also as a result has left great wealth for his family. by the *Marley* generation.

In the case of the lottery, players depend solely on luck of the draw. Unfortunately that process has not put that winner through the mill of adversity to wind up with that lucky number; it was just mainly the purchasing of a ticket which produced that result. By now it should be fully understood that success is a learned endeavor and all self-made millionaires would attest to this. No lessons learned - no graduating.

Success is not something you stumble into, it is a journey and inevitably as I mentioned before - leaves clues. Wherever you focus your attention and put your energy, that area will bring forth fruit. As you sow, you will certainly reap.

Most people who have made the luck of the draw (the lottery), unfortunately are now penniless and lack the ability to recreate that kind of wealth. Mainly because they have not gone through the growth process necessary to handle it.

When Henry Ford was asked what he'd do if he lost his fortune? He, without hesitation said that he would be a millionaire again within five years. [2]

Donald Trump, a self made billionaire at one point just about lost it all. But because he'd created his fortune he was able to turn around and recreate it himself in a short space of time. He may have taken a detour but certainly not lost his direction.

It is often said that "If you don't know where you are going any road will take you there." In the story about Alice In Wonderland, There was a point when Alice came to a fork in the road. She asked the Cheshire cat, "Would you tell me please, which way I ought to go from here?"

The cat responded, "That depends a great deal on where you want to go." Alice told him that she didn't care much. The Cat smilingly gestured, "Then it doesn't matter which way you go."

Every vision needs to have a significant purpose. You need to know what you are doing and why. Then a picture of what it will be like once you arrive. No one wants to travel to a place without a beautiful end in mind. And what matters most are the values you take with you as your daily guide. It's important to enjoy the journey towards that particular destination. [3]

Vision, the possibility of a dream coming true – moves us forward. There's something meaningful to wake up too – a journey to pursue. Peter Drucker said,

> *"The best way to predict your future is to create it."*[4]

According to Ted Turner the creator of the broadcast empire,

> *"A visionary is supposed to have a vision of the future.*[5]

Howard Schultz, saw potential in the espresso bar (Starbucks). Consequently, he was able to convince the owners to hire him. In 1982 they made him director of marketing. While on a trip to Italy he noticed that these coffee bars were on not only every block, but they served excellent espresso and served as meeting places at over 200,000 locations there.

Heading back to Seattle his plan of replicating was met with huge resistance from the owners. His idea was rejected at least 250 times. Shultz, ticked off, started his own coffee business, called Il Giomale. As a result of his successful venture, one year later he bought Starbucks for $3.8 million.

In addition to serving a great cup of coffee Schultz wanted to build a company with soul. So he insisted that all employees working more than 20 hours a week get comprehensive health care coverage – which included coverage for unmarried spouses. Plus the employee stock option plan.

Schultz, also a lover of basketball, recently bought the Seattle Supersonics for $250 million.

Asked the secret of his success, he states 4 principles.

1. Don't be threatened by people smarter than you.
2. Compromise anything but your values.
3. Renew yourself when you are hitting home runs.
4. Everything matters.[6]

I'm always reminded of many childhood experiences including watching my parents exercise their farming skills. First they prepared the land by removing the rough shrubbery, and then plowed the land. Then they sowed corn in anticipation of a harvest. After a few days the little corn plants sprouted. The corn was then watered and fertilized.

Weeds shot up attempting to destroy the now growing green acres of corn. My parents summoned us to embark on not only molding around those plants, but destroying the treacherous weeds. Like destroyers we moved in with our hoe (an iron tool used to prepare the land and remove weeds). We whacked those weeds out and laid them to rot next to the corn plants - providing fertilizer for the now aggressively growing corn. It wasn't long before ears of corn were popping up everywhere. The birds came to get fed. We were once again summoned, and moved in with sticks which we inserted into the ground and tied black plastic bags to them. These served as a deterring object which as the wind blew chased the birds away.

It was now harvest time as we picked numerous baskets of corn. My parents' vision was now a reality as those ears of corn were sold at Friday's market. Not only that, we cooked, roasted, baked and ground corn for consumption.

Ken Blanchard writes,

> *Vision generates tremendous energy, excitement, and passion because people feel they are making a difference. They know what they are doing and why.*[7]

Visionaries don't half step they see it BIG. They see opportunities where may don't. When a building is being demolished, they see a new future for where that building once stood. They see beyond the empty space, they see apartment building, office space, storage unit, just to name a few.

I attended an event about a year 2008 where visionary Robert Kiyosaki was the keynote speaker. Robert, in addition to talking about his rich dad poor dad philosophy based on his book Rich Dad Poor Dad addressed his prediction of the oncoming recession. Mr. Kiyosaki articulated the importance of accumulating wealth during its tenure and the fact that it would get much worse before it even gets better. The year 2008 was a tough year for our country economically, with a compilation of huge company bailouts, bank mergers, layoffs, unemployment now in the millions, home foreclosures, the closing of several businesses, and the rising cost of health care as well gasoline.

Any economist will tell you that it's not yet over. They will also tell you that it is the worse it has ever been since the 1929-1939 depression, and the fact remains that we have not yet experienced the bottom of it all. In my opinion if entrepreneurs and big thinkers don't step up to the plate it could be a long haul for many waiting to score financially.

What are the people with a failure mindset doing? Complaining, becoming cynical. Conversely the visionaries buckle down and search for ways to create massive wealth. Why? It's a known fact that during a recession most people sell their possessions at huge discounts in order to survive. The cost of homes has declined drastically and continues to do so. In January of 2009, I was reading through a luxury home magazine, which I later loaned it to a friend. My friend later picked out a home in Beverly Hills, California, for her dream board. At the time the home was listed at $12.5M.

A month later after church we decided to take a dream tour of it. The home was now going for $9.5M. I happen to know the seller who is a very successful Hollywood movie producer. He knew that if he didn't sell it quickly, in the next twelve months he could end up selling it for less than half of the initial list price. I returned a month later for a second tour. That house was already in escrow.

Chris Gardener had spent most of his childhood years shuffled between foster homes and other relatives, after his mother couldn't adequately support him and his other siblings any longer.
He also struggled to find his way after graduating high school. He later enlisted in the U.S. Navy with hopes of leaving the country, this dream however never materialized.

After several odd jobs, earning sometimes less than $10,000.00 a year he met a stockbroker who drove a Ferrari plus earned over $80,000.00 a month. Enthused, he decided to become a stock broker himself and went out persistently knocking on doors of investment firms hoping to find one that would give him a chance. As a result, he found himself in jail after a police officer ran his license tags and discovered $1,200 of fines in unpaid parking tickets that he owed the city.

After 10 days in jail he went directly to a job interview with Dean Witter – dirty jeans and all. The interviewer, after hearing his story, sympathized and hired him. As a result of that bold move on Chris' part, his bio has turned into what I think is one of the greatest success story in American history.

During that interim, he lost his job, his ex-girlfriend left him to raise their 18 month child alone. He also got kicked out of his home. While studying for his brokers exams, he lived in shelters and $10 a night motels with his son. As a result of his determination, he received his brokers' license and got hired by Bear Stearns. In addition his bio has made it to the big screen. *The Pursuit of Happiness*, starring Will Smith. And the rest is history for this man who kept looking forward.[8]

- What is your vision for your future?
- Have you made a dream board; What do you have listed on it?
- Is your vision something that wakes you up out of bed, excited with the zeal to dominate?

Sean, an acquaintance of mine, now in his early 30s, was over $23,000.00 in debt and lived in a garage with his fiancé Loren, without a restroom seven years ago. He got involved in a home based business. On his dream board he placed his dream car, a gray Mercedes Benz, a town house, a black and white pen along with other items.

Today, Sean has already earned close to a million dollars in passive income in addition to the gray Mercedes Benz, the town home which he totally gutted out and remodeled, and that black and white pen which he carries with him all the time. He'd hinted to me about his plan to surprise his bride on their wedding day. Last year I attended their dream wedding. In the middle of the ceremony he surprised her with the delivery of a gray hard top convertible BMW. He, an Israeli immigrant to the U.S. now enjoys spending most of his time with Loren while creating a vision for other entrepreneurs.

Humanity though sometimes anti-visionary never forgets its dreamers.

Columbus cherished the vision of another world and he discovered it. [9] Although, some didn't help fund his expedition and many others claimed that he was totally insane.
Copernicus fostered a vision of a multiplicity of worlds and a wider universe, and he revealed it.[9]

Henry Ford visualized, then designed and built his famous Model-T. And as a result, today we do not ride around on a horse and buggy.

Dr. Martin Luther King Jr. had a dream that black kids and white kids will hold hands together and it has come to pass. To quote Dr. King:

> *"If a man hasn't discovered something that he'll die for, he isn't fit to live."*[10]

What visions do you still have on the back burner that you genuinely want to accomplished? Dare yourself by bringing them forward! Dust them off! Write them down.

> *"You may be keeping accounts, and presently you shall walk out of the door that has for so long has seemed to be the barrier of your ideals, and shall find yourself before an audience-the pen still behind your*

ear, the ink stains on your fingers-and then and there shall pour out the torrent of your inspiration. You may be driving sheep, and you shall wander to the city-bucolic and openmouthed; shall wander into the studio of a great master. And after a time the great master shall say, 'I have nothing more to teach you' And now you have become the master, who did so recently dream of great things while driving sheep. You shall lay down the saw and the plane to take on the regeneration of the world."[11] Says, poet Stanton Kirkham Davis.

Our world needs men and women with vision; men who are willing to Man up and women with the tenacity of Rosa Parks.

A vision needs to be strong and unwavering; no one makes it upstream with just a mere wish. If you have a vision and envision that you can't accomplish your vision, **watch out because somebody else will**. Yikes! Tough statement but it's true. Someone else will eat your chocolate covered ice cream and smile while doing so.

What is your vision for your life?

"THE WORLD-MUCH AS WE WANT IT TO BE-DOES NOT ACCORD WITH OUR INTUITION...THOSE WHO ARE SUCCESSFUL AT CREATING SOCIAL EPIDEMICS DO NOT JUST DO WHAT THEY THINK IS RIGHT. THEY DELIBERATELY TEST THEIR INTUITIONS."

- MALCOLM GLADWELL

Chapter Six

TIMING

Timing is everything. The famous axiom states: The "T" in *timing* is better than the "T" in *talent.* If the sun misses its appointment with planet earth we could for a long time be in utter darkness. If the waves miss their timing the ocean will swallow us up.

Timing has a lot to do with synchronicity but more so with preparedness. Successful people not only are adept at preparation, they rely on their intuition to capitalize on ideas. Therefore, whenever a great opportunity presents itself they are all over it. Philosopher, Benjamin Disraeli says,

> *"The secret of success in life is for a man to be ready for his time when it comes."*

Abraham Lincoln on one of the biggest failures in his life said:

"Give me six hours to chop down a tree and I will spend the first four sharpening the axe."

Bottom line let me rephrase in case you missed it, when one is prepared and the right opportunity presents itself, he seizes it and totally dominates. That's what others call luck. In my opinion that is success at the utmost – the way a high achiever performs.

Most high achievers love what they do and are at their best doing so. They allow their creativity to operate at their max. Conversely, so many people allow their creativity to be caged up doing things they detest doing - simply because it pays the bills. I have seen people with so much potential waste it away behind a cubicle.

Today in America "leverage" the word of the wealthy has tremendous appeal. The current recession has **unveiled** this entrepreneurial mindset. This is a great example of how one can use the timing of events to their advantage. With so many layoffs people are beginning to realize that they need more than having a job. I believe that one of the blessings derived from this recession will be a major entrepreneurial revolution – producing more entrepreneurs than any other economic downturn in our nation's history. My prediction is that the people who make that mental switch by thinking outside of the cubicle will produce more wealth than many others who've gone before them.

I was recently introduced to Arri, a very ambitious man in his 30's. He made a huge fortune back in his college days in the pager business – way in the millions. At one point he almost got kicked out of his dorm because of the steady flow of clients.

Arri later sold that business to get into the cell phone business. At that time only about 2 percent of people owned cell phones. He was smart enough to place himself in-front of that trend. As a result he has not amassed great fortune, but shows what can be done when one puts him or herself at the right place at the right time.

In that business he made millions and sold it to get into the DSL business when dial up was proven to be way to slow for graphics and the much larger files. He has also dominated in that industry. Arri thrives on picking the right opportunity at the right time – he positioned himself in front of the trend rather than behind of it.

Most successful people aren't lucky; they just master the law of timing. This means, they are constantly taking action in some way or another. Are you sure you want to use your friend as an example? And My movie producer friend amassed his fortune through a string of events. After his divorce he chose to simplify his life, which helped him to move forward. It was during this time that he made his first big movie which generated over $35M. It wasn't long before he moved out of the apartment complex where he was living, and bought a house in a upscale neighborhood.

Originally, the idea for the horror film was presented to him by a rookie producer, who didn't even have an office. My friend quickly saw the potential in the project and they collaborated on making what became a very successful movie. In order to finance this movie he sold his property, put some money down on another property and used a portion to finance the film. The film has grossed over $100M in its first and subsequent installments. He used his mind-sight instead of his eyesight when he purchased that piece of property. His initial investment has now brought him over $500,000,000, within the last five years. Some said that he was lucky. I don't believe in luck. I believe that real success occurs when preparedness and opportunity meets due to timing.

In his bestseller *Rich Dad Poor Dad* - Investor and business man Robert Kiyosaki talks about being a professional investor. He claims that the number one key is to find an opportunity that someone else missed. He writes',

> *"You see with your mind what others missed with their eyes."*[4] Kiyosaki explains: *A friend bought this run down old house. It was spooky to look at. Everyone wondered why he bought it. What that man saw that we did not was that the house came with four extra empty lots. He realized that by going to the title company. After buying the house, the man tore it down and sold the five lots to a builder for three times what he paid for the entire property. As a result he made $75,000 for two months' work.*[5] He further explains: *Great opportunities are not seen with your eyes. They are seen with your mind. Most people never get wealthy simply because they are not trained financially to recognize opportunities right in front of them.* [6]

As you strive to realize your vision, expect to be criticized and or called lucky. Philosopher, James Allen explains:

> *"The thoughtless, the ignorant, and the indolent, seeing the apparent effects of things and not the things themselves, talk of luck, of fortune, and of chance. Seeing others grow rich, they say, 'How lucky they are!' Observing others become intellectual, they exclaim, 'How highly favored they*

are!' And noting the saintly character and wide influence of still others, they remark, 'How chance aids them at every turn!' They do not see the trials and failures and struggles which these people have voluntarily encountered in order to gain their experience; have no knowledge of the sacrifices they have made, of the undaunted efforts they have put forth, of the faith they have exercised, that they might overcome the apparently insurmountable and realize the vision of their heart. They do not know the darkness and the heartaches; they only see the light and joy and call it "luck," They do not see the long and arduous journey but only behold the pleasant goal and call it "good fortune." They do not understand the process but only perceive the result and call it "chance."[7]

Having a vision provides the propellant or the belief to see it come true. Keeping that vision alive though, is imperative, because there's always going to be the naysayer(s) who will tell you that you don't have what it takes to make it a reality. Sometimes, if it is a close friend or relative they will certainly remind you of those skeletons in your closet.-eliminate the sentence You may excitedly launch your ship and understand that those winds and storms are going to come billowing against you. Trusting their possible caring attitude, you can make that mistake of lending a deaf ear to your unused capacity crying out within you saying "**You can do it**!" So many missed opportunities occur from failure to listen to that still small voice. That voice, like a great friend prodding an individual on through the tough times. Those times when others lose belief in *them*.

Let's face it, in order to be successful you will need to go through the cocoon stage in order to change. Unsuccessful people remain out of sync with success mainly because they resist change. Ask any winner and they'll tell you the major difference between successful people and unsuccessful people is successful people master the art of bouncing back from failure. They keep on keeping on. They continue to change and adapt to new circumstances.

Do you know someone who started something but failed to finish? Someone who got straight "A's" now all they get are "F's"? I know so many would be authors who begin writing a book, yet they never finish. It never makes its way out of their computer hard drive. They live a life of "if only I can or I wish I did." Don't fall into that trap; it's always fully baited with excuses, waiting for failures bent on quitting. Launch your dream and pursue it with reckless abandon. Harriet Beecher Stowe declared:

> *"When you get into a tight place and everything*
> *goes against you, 'til it seems as though you could*

not hold on a minute longer. Never give up then, for that is just the place and time that the tide will turn." [8]

Back in my prewriting days, I could have said *"Let that major movie studio keep their film, do whatever they want to do with it. In Hollywood it's all a rat race mindset anyway. I wasn't meant to be a writer in the first place. I came here only to act so I'll sit and wait for the auditions. No one wants to read about what I have to say. I'm a high school dropout and on and on..."* Instead it was perfectly timed, a blessing in disguise – I heeded that call to write. That hunch has propelled me into the driver's seat. In *The Tipping Point,* Malcolm Gladwell states:

"The world-much as we want it to be-does not accord with our intuition...Those who are successful at creating social epidemics do not just do what they think is right. They deliberately test their intuitions." [1]

If you were to interview the most successful people in the world, they would tell you that one of the keys to their overwhelming success is that they trusted their hunch. Yes, it's like fishing; they felt the nibble and tugged on the line.

I believe that when you are given a vision, you are also given the ability, and with proper timing, you'll certainly reach your destination if you persevere.

How's your timing?

"NOTHING IN THE WORLD CAN TAKE THE PLACE OF PERSISTENCE. TALENT WILL NOT. NOTHING IN THE WORLD IS MORE COMMON THAN UNSUCCESSFUL PEOPLE WITH TALENT. GENIUS WILL NOT. UNREWARDED GENIUS IS ALMOST A PROVERB. EDUCATION WILL NOT. THE WORLD IS FULL OF EDUCATED DERELICTS. PERSISTENCE, DETERMINATION AND HARD WORK MAKE THE DIFFERENCE."

— CALVIN COOLIDGE

Chapter Seven

DETERMINATION

We've now come to one of the most important chapters in this book. This embodies the defining quality between people who succeed and the ones who don't. **You know yourself and the potential inside, you have a purpose, you have developed passion, acquired a magnetic personality, created a vision for your life and found the right time to launch it. You leave no road for retreat. In other words "you burn the ships" the bridge gets demolished. There's no way out. Therefore, success becomes inevitable.**

In *Think and Grow Rich*, Napoleon Hill recounts this story:

> A great warrior was faced with a situation which made it necessary for him to make a decision which ensured him success on the battlefield. This leader was about to send his armies against a powerful foe, whose men

fearfully outnumbered his. He got busy and loaded his soldiers in boats, sailed to the enemy's country, unloaded soldiers and equipment. Then he gave the orders to burn the ships that had carried them. Addressing his men before the first battle, he said "You see the boats going up in smoke. That means that we cannot leave these shores alive unless we win! We now have no choice-*we win*-or *we perish!*" They won.[2]

All successful people have in common this particular trait. They have learned how to develop the habit of perseverance towards setting and reaching their goals. Their "not giving up mindset and philosophy" separates them from the rest of the world. They know that without determination they will never arrive at their destination. So they persist in spite of the obstacles which are presented along the way. They become masters of the art of getting back up when they get knocked down.

In order to succeed in today's world and make a difference one needs to not only learn from their successes but also from their failures. One ought to be able to look back at those diametrically opposed experiences and say "This is what I did in order to succeed and this is what I've learned. This is what I did that caused me to fail and this is what I've learned. "

Determination has so much to do with strong faith. Faith is described as "the evidence of things not seen." Determination calls for a strong, unwavering faith, one capable of moving mountains along the way.

I moved to Hollywood, California in July 1996 as an actor. Within those first two years I landed nine TV commercials in a thirteen month span. I then experienced a journey dominated by failures. **So much that, constantly being beaten up by life in Hollywood led me to believe that every seed that I planted was killed by haters and player haters alike. Those industry pythons who made it their duty to destroy the kernels before they grew up much less bear fruit.** They delighted in squeezing my dreams out of me. Never! They had it coming. I decided that I was going to start believing in myself.

I knew where I came from and where I wanted to go. The boy from the islands of **Saint Vincent and the Grenadines,** who, went to school at times without shoes on his feet? I had had enough and was going from here on to make a significant difference. What I touched had to turn to gold. Dare the ones who tried to stop me or get in the way. I was like a rhino coming through. Failure wasn't going to be an alternative. I was going through whatever stood in my way, en-route to my destiny.

While I had written several screenplays, I had always wanted to etch my first book. I felt that I had very unique stories to share. So, on January 21st, 2007 after having a heart to heart, a mind over matter interlude with my hidden guide and mentor the late Dr. Martin Luther King Jr., I took that tremendous leap of faith. As I looked at his picture several times, reflecting on what he stood for, if only I could do 20 % of what he stood for I'd be very happy. Releasing just one percent of my untapped potential could make a significant difference in the world. So I launched out and wrote my first book, *The 5 Steps To Changing Your Life*. Believing that I had what it took to write it.

While pondering my own legacy, I knew that I had not done enough for mankind and myself. I stared at MLK's quote:

> *"Take the first step in faith, you don't have to see the whole staircase. Just take the first step."*[3]

For well over 30 minutes, consumed by it and all that he stood for, I passionately outlined my first book *The 5 Steps to Changing Your Life.*

My contribution towards changing mindsets at this point took center stage. If I could help to change the mindset and philosophy of one dream deprived individual, this world would become a better place I reasoned.

So, through inspiration I was moved to write my first book. That night I opened up my writing software, outlined the first draft and begun writing my first book. I felt as if a dam of inspiration was released from my mind. I kept going back and forth to my book library looking for quotes to supplement my written thoughts. There, I was able to retrieve books which I had previously read. I scanned through their pages, locating the exact high-lighted quote necessary for insert into my waiting text. I felt possessed with - the Michael Jordan like feeling when he dumped 69 points on the Cleveland Cavaliers. Inspiration took over and I passionately completed the first draft of that volume in one week.

An editor and cover designer stepped up to the plate as if summoned by some unknown guide. I must admit that I spoke with several designers over a 3 month span who'd promised to work with me on the project but never did. Finally the right one showed up. He found exactly the image I was looking for and the book was published in June of 2007. My book was released and made available on Amazon and at other online stores. I was ecstatic!

One of my clients at that time, a well known celebrity who I chauffeured, learned about my new book and promised to give me a "blurb" after reading it. The book was delivered as requested. I waited for the blurb and have never heard back from her since. Nevertheless, my book received endorsements from other sources. Meanwhile my boss, who was her good friend, pulled the cord on me - I was out of a job. **He'd heard my sirens coming and knew that my mindset and philosophy was not that of a settler.**

These turn of events wasn't because of a failed marriage but someone who couldn't see success for himself. Therefore, he didn't want it for me. In addition my roommate at the time said he didn't need the money but I had taken so many of his excuses away during our dwelling together. He couldn't stand my velocity; he knew that with my tenacity I'd out-work anybody. While he slept I wrote. Consequently, after weeks of unemployment I once again found myself homeless. A situation I detested and was unprepared for. YET I WAS NOT GOING TO BE DENIED! I WAS DETERMINED TO BECOME AN AUTHOR REGARDLESS OF MY CIRCUMSTANCES.

Back in 2007, while my editor edited my first book, I started writing *Keep Love Alive*. I later titled the volume *Spread Some Love (Relationships 101)* in order to cover the basics on relationships. Martin Luther King day the next year (2008) rolled around and I was once again haunted by my lack of accomplishments in life thus far. In spite of my recurring adversity, on MLK day of 2008 I printed out the first completed draft of my new book. With all the time management skills I'd gleaned through the years, without inspiration, I don't know if I could have pulled that off. Inspiration led me to action once again and I created my own break instead of sitting around looking for it. I felt like I was born to write.

In early April 2008 I founded my own publishing company, Books That Will Enhance Your Life. I published the Amazon kindle edition of the book. A few weeks later the e-book and paperback versions were published and released thereafter.

Upon receiving the proof of *Spread Some Love (Relationships 101).* I kissed it several times. A friend was with me at the time and jokingly said, "You kissed yourself" For those of you who have seen the book you will notice that I've used one of my headshots on the front cover. To him I replied "Yes." If only he knew how much value I saw in this product. I knew that I had brought something of significance to the world.

A bookstore chain refused from stocking my book on their shelves. They flat out said "We are not going to carry that title because the author published it through a small independent publisher." and additionally "it didn't fit our model." That ticked me off because (a) I founded and owned that publishing company *Books That Will Enhance Your Life* and (b) I wrote the book in addition to owning the rights to it. That didn't sit too well with me, so I went undercover.

Their booksellers claimed that it was not modeled for their store. Well, based on my research, I found out that if a store really wanted to carry a book as long as it was available from one of the major distributors and was returnable, they could shortlist that book. But instead they were saying flat out that they were not going to carry the title, "why?" I pried further.

By this time I had refused from taking their "No" for an answer. In less than three weeks after doing my research and going on a tirade with them, they stocked my book in several of their California bookstores. That led to more stores following suite on the East Coast. When someone said no I purposefully pushed for the YES and got it.

Through Word Of Mouth marketing my book had already arrived on shelves not only in California but also on the East coast as well. So much that the constant flow of orders from that particular title alerted their corporate office according to their spokesperson. My sub publisher contacted me to make sure there had not been any fraud involved.

As far as I knew people were just flat out ordering copies of the book. My phone line was burning up with inquiries about this new title. Friends were telling other friends about it just like a good movie. WOM marketing had the advantage. The small press acquisition department for that book chain dragged their feet with my title submission for national distribution. – in the meantime I'd already secured my first major book-signing event with one of their local stores.

The upcoming signing was creating such a buzz, so much that a major entertainment TV station proposed to cover me along with the event. However, they pulled out one day before the event. They claimed that they weren't able to get a host interviewer to cover for that weekend. I immediately got on the phone and organized my own camera crew. Even a freelance stylist provided her services on my behalf.

The day arrived. I showed up excited and dressed to the nines, after all it was my first major book signing event. All eyes were on me. The very inspirational on-camera interview ended, and then it was on to the book signing event. In less than a few hours all the books they had in stock were sold out much to the surprise of their management team. Their cash registers were going Cha Ching – Cha Ching - Cha Ching. I watched as "Spread Some Love (Relation-ships 101)" exited in shopping bags.

Those results still did not influence the small press into a nationwide - in - store placement of the volume. They came up with every worn out excuse under the sun including me possibly trying a later resubmission of the title.

While they were dealing with indecision at that department surrounding acquisition of my book, the visionary in me operated at full throttle. I was busy creating the script for a docu-drama based on the book. The book had already sold thousands of copies without any publicity within the first four months. It was already apparent to me that people were hungry relationally. Therefore, no matter how long the current recession lasted, I knew that relationship minded individuals were still going to be working on their relationships. I continued to move forward with

my writing, and in addition produced my docu-
drama based on relationships.

IT COULDN'T BE DONE

Somebody said it couldn't be done,
But he with a chuckle replied
That "maybe it couldn't," but he would be one
Who wouldn't say till he'd tried,

So he buckled right in with the trace of a grin
On his face. If he worried, he'd hid it.
Somebody scoffed: "Oh, you'll never do that;
At least no one ever has done it.
But he took off his coat and he took off his hat,

And the first thing we know he begun it.
With a lift of his chin and a bit of a grin,
Without any doubting or "quiddit"
He started to sing as he tackled the thing

That couldn't be done, and he did it.
There are thousands to tell you it cannot be
done,
There are thousands to prophesy failure;
There are thousands to point out to you one by
one;

The dangers that wait to assail you.

But just buckle in with a bit of a grin,
Just take off your coat and go to it
Just start in to sing as you tackle the thing
That "cannot be done" and you'll do it.

--Unknown

In *The 5 Steps To Changing Your Life* I also recounted the persistency of one of America's biggest failures. It would have been so easy for this young man to bow his head in shame and give up.

> *He failed in business in 1831, he was defeated for the legislature in '32, he was elected to the legislature in '34, his sweetheart died in '35, he had a nervous breakdown in '36, he was defeated for Speaker in '38, he was defeated for elector in '40, he was defeated for Congress in '43, he was elected to Congress in '48, he was defeated for the Senate in '50, and he was defeated for Vice President in '56 and for the Senate in '58. But in 1860, he was elected President of the United States. His name was Abraham Lincoln.*[4] A major contributor to civil rights.

You will find that most successful people have all encountered failure along their path to success. Some many times, others hundreds of times, while some ranked as high as in thousands of times – as in the case of Thomas A. Edison. The most important element in their accomplishment is that they never gave up. Once again another example of determination to succeed.

Any successful person will tell you that it takes focus, strong character and determination in order to succeed. This applies to all areas of their lives. Several years ago after my divorce, I got immersed into the subject of relationships and have written several books on the subject since. I've noticed that many people work hard on their jobs and not on their relationships. As a result they end up in divorce and wonder why their marriage hasn't worked. They missed the embodiment of this chapter you are now reading. Determination starts with knowing that you have what it takes to succeed.

Are you ready for the climb amidst the turbulence in order to acquire success?

How is your thought process?

This is one of my favorite poems because it sums up my philosophy on determination.

If you think you are beaten, you are,
If you think you dare not, you don't.

If you like to win, but you think you can't,
It is almost certain you won't.
If you think you'll lose, you are lost,
For out in this world we find,
Success begins with a fellow's will-
It's all in the state of mind.

If you think you are outclassed, you are,
You've got to think high to rise,
You've got to be sure of yourself before
You can ever win a prize.

Life's battles don't always go
To the stronger or faster man,
But soon or late the man who wins
Is the man WHO THINKS HE CAN!

-    Unknown

Most people never get to experience the other 90% of their potential. They never experience the thrill of sweet success. They fear getting knocked down. Nobody has ever accomplished anything worthwhile without being tested and tried. Successful people are winners; they let nothing stand in their way of victory. You can smell their tenacity like expensive cologne because they have a feeling of their own worth. They think: I can. I will and I shall not be denied.

The power of your purpose depends on the vigor and determination behind it. And your determination is necessary to take that ball into the end zone and score that winning touchdown.

First you have to believe though, really believe that you can become successful before you do. "We do not attract that which we want but that which we are."5 It has to be a mindset. And success is a process which takes patience. We live in a microwave age where everything is instant. Instant this and instant that. Well, there is no such thing as instant success. Success is never like the Jack and the Beanstalk scenario. It is never a fairy tale but the complete opposite. It is a Farming 101 mindset – sowing and reaping.

Sometimes other people don't see what we do while we are in the trenches in order to acquire our success. Most times they only see the end result and mistakenly call it luck.

I am always reminded of how a Chinese bamboo tree whenever I think about determination. Success calls for great determination. Ask any successful person.

> *You take a little seed and plant, water, and fertilize it for a whole year, and nothing happens.*

The second year you water and fertilize it, and nothing happens.

The third year you water and fertilize it, and nothing yet.

The fourth year you water and fertilize it, and still nothing.

The fifth year you continue to water and fertilize the seed. Sometime during the fifth year, the Chinese bamboo tree sprouts and grows NINETY FEET IN SIX WEEKS.

Most often success is like that Chinese bamboo tree, requiring you to hang in there much longer before seeing the fruits of your labor. Many misunderstand the process and view success like throwing on a superman outfit – such a temporary ordeal. Don't be mistaken, it goes much deeper than that. No wonder it becomes unnervingly uncomfortable for most failures to be in the presence of the successful for too long because that successful person quickly takes their excuses away.

According to Malcolm Gladwell in his book *Outliers*

"What is the question we always ask about the successful? We want to know what they're like –

what kind of personalities they have, or how intelligent they are, or what kind of lifestyles they have, or what special talents they might have been born with. And we assume that it is those personal qualities that explain how that individual reached the top."[6] He continues: *"In the autobiographies published every year by the billionaire/entrepreneur/rock star/celebrity, the story line is always the same: our hero is born in modest circumstances and by virtue of his own grit and talent fights his way to greatness."* [7]

Let me introduce you

Michael Phelps made it a habit of working out in the pool for 8 hours a day for several years in order to accomplish Olympic excellence.

We find that failure contributes greatly to one's success. Michael Jordan, the greatest player to ever play the game of basketball addressed failing this way,

> *"I've missed more than 9,000 shots in my career, I've lost almost 300 games. Twenty six times I've been trusted to take the game winning shot and missed. I have failed over and over and over in my life. And that's why I succeed!"* [8]

When we think of Michael Jordan, we remember him as "Air Jordan" with these stats: Six-time NBA champion (1991-93, 1996-98); MVP (1988, '91, '92, '96, '98); 10-time All-NBA First Team (1987-93, 1996-98) etc. Memories of his failures aren't foremost on our minds we just remember his achievements. For most of us we can still see him with his tongue hanging out as he took the ball to the hoop.

In grade school Albert Einstein was a very unimpressive student. So much that the when his dad asked the headmaster what profession his young son should pursue, the headmaster replied, "It doesn't matter, because he will never make success in anything."[9] The rest is historic. Einstein became one of the greatest physicists of the 20th century. His persistence developed in him the natural gifts of genius.

The Wright brothers, Orville and Wilbur wanted to construct a machine that flew. People believed that it was highly impossible. "How do you keep that thing up there? Never, it's impossible!" They questioned. In addition, while the two brothers were busily pursuing their invention, scientific studies were carried out to prove that a body heavier than air could not possibly fly. Because of their success we now travel in an airplane for duration of over twelve hours in the sky across several continents.

She was referred to as "Moses" not only by the hundreds of slaves she helped to freedom, but also by the thousands of others she inspired. Because of her commitment to a cause Harriet Tubman became the most famous leader of the Underground Railroad to aid slaves escaping the Free states or Canada.

Her first expedition took place in 1851, when she managed to thread her way through the backwoods to Baltimore and return to the North with her sister and her sister's children. From that time until the onset of the Civil War, she traveled to the South about 18 times and helped close to 300 slaves escape. In 1857, led her parents to freedom in Auburn, New York, and resided there.

Tubman was never caught and never lost a slave to the Southern militia. As her reputation grew, so too did the desire among Southerners to put a stop to her activities. Rewards for her capture once totaled about $40,000, a lot of money in those days. During the Civil War, Tubman served as a nurse, scout, and sometime-spy for the Union army, mainly in South Carolina. She also took part in a military campaign that resulted in the rescue of 756 slaves and destroyed millions of dollars' worth of enemy property.

After the war, Tubman returned to Auburn and continued her involvement in social issues, including the women's rights movement. In 1908, she established a home in Auburn for elderly and indigent blacks that later became known as the Harriet Tubman Home. She died on March 10, 1913, at approximately age of 93.[10]

Tubman's passionate commitment of love for her people kept her going back until every slave was freed, regardless of the dangers involved.

The foregoing people are normal like you and me, though because of their own uniqueness they acquired their own unique brand of success. They were driven by an extra-ordinary determination to achieve their goals at all costs. Every opposition brought them closer to a "YES." They are adept at turning setbacks into comebacks.

> *"Nothing in the world can take the place of persistence. Talent will not. Nothing is more common than unsuccessful men with talent. Genius will not. Unrewarded genius is almost a proverb. Education will not. The world is full of educated derelicts. Persistence, determination and hard work make the difference."*
>
> — Calvin Coolidge

Persistence and determination! These special character traits ought to be embodied in the legacy we
pass on to our children. It's a common trend that
children tend to develop their relationship values
from their parents. And those qualities they pass on to
their future generations.

Here is an example of a tradition passed on. A new
bride was one day making dinner for her husband. He
noticed that she cut off both ends of the ham before
putting it in the saucepan. He was taken aback and
asked: Why such a move?

She responded that her mom always cut off the ends
of the ham before cooking it, making it very delicious.
One day while he was with her mother he asked her
why she cut off the ends of the ham before cooking it.
She said she didn't know and that she saw her mom
do it that way and it was delicious.

One day while with his wife's grandma he pried
further about this ham cooking process. She said,

> *"I cut the ends off my ham because it was too big to
> fit in my small roasting pan. It has nothing to do
> with the taste and texture. I had to cut the ends out
> of the ham to get it to fit in my pan!"*

Just because someone else did it doesn't mean you should do it too because of tradition.

- Are you determined enough to make a difference?
- Will you create a new lineage of future champions with your values.

In the words of author Berton Braley:

> *"If you want a thing bad enough to go out and fight for it, to work day and night for it, to give up your time, and your sleep for it...if all that you dream and scheme is about it, and life seems useless and worthless without it...if you gladly sweat for it and fret for it and plan for it and lose all you terror of opposition for it...if you simply go after that thing you want with all of your capacity, strength and sagacity, faith, hope and confidence and stern pertinacity...if neither cold, poverty, famine, nor gout, sickness nor pain, of body and brain, can keep you away from the thing that you want...if dogged and grim you beseech it, with the help of God, you WILL get it!"*[11]

Ask any successful person and they'll tell you that going through those walls towards their destiny took persistence and strong determination to succeed. But once they broke through, their life like that of the beautiful butterfly emerging from the cocoon became enhanced.

How determined are you to become successful?

"LIFE IS BIGGER THAN FOOTBALL OR BASKETBALL BUT THE SAME RULES MAINTAIN. IF YOU KEEP STRONG, PHYSICALLY FIT, FULL OF ENERGY AND ENTHUSIASM, YOU ARE THE MAN WHOM LIFE'S COACH IS GOING TO PICK WHEN THE WINNING TOUCHDOWN IS NEEDED."

– WILLIAM DANFORTH.

Chapter Eight

BALANCE

Successful individuals deserve a well rounded life. After all, the price paid for success is very significant. Therefore life should be enjoyed to the fullest. The social, mental, physical, and spiritual areas of one's life should not go neglected by someone desiring success. For those desiring a long life - practice moderation in everything you do.

Learning to smell the roses along the way is of utmost importance for anyone wanting to be successful. Some people work all the time and find no time to play or do anything fun. I'm not talking about putting aside what needs to get done in order to succeed. I'm talking about the importance of taking care of all areas of one's life. Having money and poor health or no relationships or no spiritual foundation or being depressed are some symptoms of an unbalanced life whether successful or not.

Many would-be-successes spend most of their time having a blast and wonder why they are not as successful as they can be.

On the other hand some work all the time just because of the income potential and spend very little time working on their relationships. As a result, those relationships may collapse. It's important to have people in your life who are supportive and are there for you along the path. It's good to have fun and laughter as well as focus and determination.

One's mental health is really important. It will be your thoughts and beliefs that can be your enemy or friend. What we think often drives our actions. Athletes in particular know the power of affirmation and visualization. They see the end in mind, their words and actions match. Lance Armstrong affirmed health and saw himself winning another Tour de France while being treated for cancer. He then came back on to win that race a total of **7 times!**

An example I find very powerful is the following that shows how a person's mental attitude can overcome the odds. A few years ago, my senior pastor's wife Holly, was diagnosed with breast cancer. Though our church believes in miracles and the power of prayer, we watched her fight this disease with the power of words. I saw her a few times during her illness and found out that she carried around index cards with words of affirmation; she didn't want anything to do with the sometimes fatal disease. Prayers were poured out on her behalf, and it's believed that she totally affirmed her own healing. Today, she travels all over the world teaching people the power of words over sickness in the body. You cannot speak both sickness and disease and expect to walk in good health.

MB, a young man in his mid-20s, moved from Northern California to Hollywood over a year ago in pursuit of the Hollywood dream. He is another example of the power of mental affirmation and determination. I met him at our church while he was still getting acclimated and we created a bond; he has admirable leadership potential. As most people who move to the entertainment industry capital know, you take the job you can get until you get the job you want. So, he took a management position at a retail store, a job which demanded him showing up to work on Sundays. I could tell he was burnt out Sunday after Sunday.

MB told me that he had had enough and was ready to move on. I saw him a week later after that conversation and he mentioned that he would be interviewing with one of the top talent agencies in the industry. He was confident about landing the job. He said, "I'm going to get it." I was a little hesitant and suggested an alternative agency just in case. He looked me dead in the eye and said "John, I'm going to get it." He said this with confidence and determination. A few days later my phone rang. It was MB and he had gotten the job. MB spoke what he wanted and got it. His reaping had much to do with his sowing; using the right mental attitude and words.

You cannot expect to speak both success and failure and create your dream. What you think of yourself you become, what you speak you do. Be conscious of your thoughts and words. Feed yourself the breakfast of champions: I am smart, I do know how to do this, I CAN do anything I set out to accomplish, I deserve to be successful...you get the point.

It seems today in America, our teens are not physically healthy. Obesity is at an all time high, leaving experts extremely concerned as the rate of juvenile diabetes rises too. On your path to success make sure to build in the time and habits to take care of yourself. This means healthy eating, getting enough sleep, daily exercise, and managing your stress. Be aware your body is your car. What are you filling it with? The fuel you use is what will allow you to continue moving forward. Exercise is vital to keeping the body fit. Your mental alertness comes from the eating a healthy balanced diet-junk food is not fuel! It provides short term burst of energy, not long term health. Start today by making healthy food choices, moving your body and managing your stress so you can become all your truly capable of being.

When it comes to spiritual health, this means many things to many people. For some, it is about meditating daily, or attending church, or being part of a community outreach. In this book we are talking about how you connect to that higher source/power that is available to all of us. It is this source, when connected to, that inspiration flows. Inspiration means "the act of inspiring; quality or state of being inspired." The ideas & thoughts that seem to be random are those coming from one's source of inspiration-whatever you choose to call it. As there are many names for this source. We sometimes have to find a way to tap into that source. It can be done through a variety of ways; some experience it while on a run, others sit in silence, or journal daily, others when listening to music, or when in prayer and meditation. Do whatever works for you. The important step is to exercise that habit and tap into **YOUR** inspired place of ideas. We all have access to this source of inspiration. Successful people develop this habit because of the ideas they receive, take action on propelling themselves forward to their destiny.

Living a balanced life requires paying attention to ones social, mental, physical and spiritual aspects. It takes daily discipline to attend to these areas. It takes a commitment to develop and use habits that support being healthy on all levels. Some days may be more balanced than others; keep at it, it'll come together. The important thing is to be aware of your habits and especially your thoughts and the words you use. Thoughts lead to words which lead to actions which = character.

Here are affirmations to use if you so choose:
➢ I am destined to succeed.
➢ I am an ever evolving person; growing and learning new things daily.
➢ I am open to opportunities, people and resources that guide me closer to my dream.
➢ I am healthy!
➢ I am making healthy choices in each moment.
➢ I am surrounded by people who believe in me.
➢ I am conscious of my thoughts, words and actions.
➢ I believe in myself!

Why are words so powerful and contribute to our success or failure? They govern our hearts and control our body on all levels - steering us toward our desired goals and dreams. Even if your life is one filled with negativity you can make that change. The ball is always in your hands. Be mindful of what you think, say and do.

When we take care of the mental, physical, social and spiritual aspects of our lives, we are not only creating balance but showing our gratitude for being wonderfully made and totally equipped to fulfill our destiny.

WHAT ARE YOU DOING TO CREATE BALANCE IN ALL AREAS OF YOUR LIFE?

"ANYONE WHO DOESN'T REALLY KNOW WHAT HE OR SHE WANTS TO DO AND DOESN'T ESTABLISH CLEAR-CUT GOALS WILL FIND IT HARD TO SUCCEED."[1]

- MARK FISHER

Chapter Nine

FULFILLING YOUR DESTINY

If you have gotten this far by now you should be feeling totally equipped and fully loaded to set your sails toward your destiny. What is your port of call? Every ship has a destination. Could you imagine a ship wandering on the sea going nowhere? In order to get where you want, you need to know what you want and go for it amidst the storms of life. **Your destiny has nothing to do with other people's opinion**. It has to do with you. Most people have an entitlement mindset. They not only think that the world owes them something but that the world, not them, needs to change.

Successful people not only ask themselves: Where do I want to go in my life and career but what do I want to become? Is your destiny well defined? I hope by now that you've found that "cause" greater than yourself and are ready to make it happen. If not, you may not ready for the quest and might want to reread this book before proceeding any further; repetition has proven to be a very important element of success.

We all have a divine untapped power, capable of guiding us towards fulfilling our destiny. Some, not yet successful may reason: "Where is it? How come "I" have never experienced it?" Do you believe in electricity? I remember growing up as a kid. In those early days we didn't have electricity. When the power supply finally came to our area I was in my late teens and like most boys with an experimental mindset decided to look for what I couldn't see – electricity. One day the perfect opportunity arose as the need to have light in our factory became apparent. So I decided to run an extension wire from our kitchen to the factory only a few yards away. I removed the screws from the light socket, looking inside there was no evidence of electricity just one black and one red wire. But when my hand inadvertently touched the red wire, my arm was almost pulled out of its socket a few times in a matter of seconds. I couldn't see the electricity but you better believe it was there in that socket. Evidence of success seems lacking in our lives mainly because we have not yet defined our destiny.

When you know who you are, you would realize that you have within the power to become the co-creator of your entire world. Let me explain. **Self knowledge is your power.** When the newly discovered you emerge, you are able to manage the circumstances of your life more readily. Your image of self becomes enhanced; you step out of your comfort zone and into the game of life. You see what you lack and begin to participate in your reconstruction process.

Ask any successful person and they will tell you that there was a point right after their self discovery process that they knew beyond a shadow of a doubt that they were going to become successful. They could almost taste it. They will also tell you that once they became focused on their destiny they refused to let any powers within them lie dormant. They dug it up and operated on full throttle. At that point they knew where they wanted to go in life. They had found their destiny – their true calling.

Successful people understand the law of momentum, knowing that it's hard to acquire and easy to lose. So whenever this awesome force is present they use it to accomplish their quantum leap. Thereby they become unstoppable in the eyes of many.

Yes "**We are powerful beyond measure.**" How do we know that? Through self discovery! When self is discovered, we move beyond our limitations and as a result we become unstoppable towards fulfilling our destiny. The detours along the way become minuscule because we've learned to trust ourselves and source of inspiration. And because of our faith, we are able to turn our defeats into victories.

We each have a destiny to fulfill and it's up to us if we reject or accept that calling. I believe that we all have been given a "cause" and guides along the way to assist us on our journey. Have you ever been on the road to a destination, got lost, and immediately found someone placed in your path as if by design to help you get back on the right track?

Yet most of us lack the ability to start because we're not sure we'll arrive.
Each of us has a calling. What you do with your calling is largely dependable on your commitment to completing life's puzzle. You could be holding on to that missing piece. Don't allow it to decay in your hands. We all are here working together. Mark Fisher writes in the book *How to be a Millionaire,*

> *"Anyone who doesn't really know what he or she wants to do and doesn't establish clear-cut goals will find it hard to succeed."*[1]

Our contribution is imperative in order to make this world a better place. When our journey here is ended would it be one which served as a blessing to humanity? Or would it be one that your grand children don't even remember your name, or no one benefits because you came. In the words of Ralph Waldo Emerson,

> "Do not go where the path may lead, go instead where there is no path and leave a trail."[2]

Self made millionaire T. Harv Eker who went from zero to a millionaire in only two and a half years, writes in his book *Secrets of The Millionaire Mind,*

> "Becoming rich isn't as much about getting rich financially as about whom you have become, in character and mind, to get rich."[3] He further states, "The fastest way to get rich and stay rich is to work on developing you! The idea is to grow yourself into a 'successful' person. Again your outer world is merely a reflection of your inner world. You are the root; your results are the fruits."[4]

I want to close by sharing an excerpt from a story as told by his wife about the man who pioneered the personal development industry. Let me introduce you to Earl Nightingale.

Earl Nightingale was born during economically depressed times. As a child because they were so poor Earl desperately wanted to know why some people grew up to enjoy prosperity. While, others, like his family struggled merely to survive. Unable to find answers to his questions from grown ups, he began reading everything he could believing that someone, somewhere had the answer.

When Earl was 35 years old he'd written and record a message. It was to be played one Saturday morning to a small group of salespeople during his absence. When Earl returned he learned that the message had made such a positive impact on the men, they wanted copies to share with their friends and families. He arranged with Columbia records to duplicate the record to meet their many requests. Much to his surprise in very little time, without any real advertising or marketing, over a million copies have been sold and he received a gold record. Earl called the message "The Strangest Secret." And this single recording was the seedling from which the entire personal development industry grew. And because he had discovered the true meaning of The Strangest Secret, which determines the outcome of one's life, he went from poverty to become one of the most highly recognized voices and name throughout the United States and from the West Indies to South Africa.

People around the world have attributed The Strangest Secret as the one message which has positively affected their lives.[5]

If one hundred ambitious teenagers were to grasp the concepts outlined in this volume and dared to make a difference it could change the economic structure of this country and the world at large. It would be well worth it. The value brought to our country by that many successful individuals would be astounding. There's an over-whelming need for people to step off the side-lines and into the game. Are you one of them? DO YOU DARE TO MAKE A DIFFERENCE?

Notes

1. Marianne Williamson
    http://thinkexist.com/quotation/as_we_let_our_light_shine-we_consciously_give/341050.html

Introduction

1. Martin Luther King Jr.
    www.brainyquote.com/quotes/m/martinluth115056.html
2. Ibid. dontknowmuch.com/kids/mlk.html
3. Harland Stoncipher, Pre-Paid Legal Services. Inc.
4. Oprah Winfrey - Bio. www.answers.com/topic/oprah-winfrey
5. Philip & Holly Wagner. 2009, Oasisla.org

Chapter 1

1. William Danforth, *I Dare You* (St. Louis: American Youth Foundation, 1991), X.
1. Gerald Sindell, The Genius Machine, Novato, New World Library, 2009), 66
2. Warren Bennis, *On Becoming a Leader*, Inc. Ontario & New York, Addison-Wesley Publishing Company, 19890, 54
3. Mahatma Gandhi, thinkexist.com/quotation/be_the_change_you _want_to_see_in_the_world...

Chapter 2

1. Ken Blanchard, Leading At A Higher Level, Prentice Hall, New Jersey, 2007, 280
2. Rick Warren, The Purpose Driven Life, Grand Rapids, Zondervan, 2002), 319
3. Napoleon Hill, The Master Key To Riches/Your Magic Power To Be Rich, New York, Penguin Group, 2007), 363
4. James Allen, *As a Man Thinketh* (New York: Bantam Books Inc., 1982),
5. Julia Cameron, The Artist's Way, New York, Tatcher/Putman. 1992), 66
6. Ibid. 66
7. Mark Fisher/Marc Allen, How To Think Like A Millionaire, Novato, New World Library, 1997), 72 (Ibid)
8. Colonel Sanders. www.articlesbase.com/entrepreneurship-articles/colonel-sanders-story-of-entrepreneurship-1000394.html
9. J.Paul Getty. www.zeromillion.com/srs-j-paul-getty

Chapter 3

1. http://thinkexist.com/quotation/develop_a_passion_for_learning-if_you_do-you_will/10266.html
2. William Danforth, I Dare You, 5
3. BillGates'Bio.http://Inventors.about.com/od/gstartinventors/a./Bill_gates.html

4. Rosa Parks. Live My Passion,
   http://www.livemypassion.com/thoughts.htm

Chapter 4

1. John Maxwell, Becoming A Person Of Influence, Nashville, Thomas Nelson Publishers, 1997), 7
2. Brian Tracy, Millionaire Habits, Entrepreneur Press, 2006) xi, xii
3. Ibid. 196

Chapter 5

1. BrainyQuote.
   www.brainyquote.com/quotes/quotes/j/johnfkenn132742.html
2. Mark Fisher/Marc Allen, How To Think Like A Millionaire, 64
3. Ken Blanchard, Leading At A Higher Level, 25
4. Ibid, 22
5. Mark Fisher/Marc Allen, How To Think Like A Millionaire, 71
6. Howard Schultz's Bio.
   www.myprimetime.com/work/ge/shultzbio/
7. Ken Blanchard, Leading At A Higher Level, 25
8. Chris Gardener – Bio.
   http://www.evancarmichael.com/Famous-Entrepreneurs/815/Chris-Gardner-Bio.html
9. Allen, *As a Man Thinketh*, revision. JMW Group Inc. New York, Published by Penguin Group,

2008), 110.
10. Ibid, 110
11. Life of Dr. King,
www.webstar.co.uk/~ubugaje/**luther**3.html
12. Allen, *As a Man Thinketh*, 40,41

Chapter 6

1. Malcom Gladwell, The Tipping Point, New York/Boston, Back Bay Books, 2000), 258
2. Benjamin Disraeli.
www.brainyquote.com/quotes/b/benjamindi134331.html
3. Abraham Lincoln.
www.brainyquote.com/quotes/a/abrahamlin109275.html
4. Robert kiyosaki, Rich Dad Poor Dad, New York/Boston, Business Plus, Hachette Book Group, 1997), 126
5. Ibid, 126
6. Ibid, 125
7. James Allen, As A Man Thinketh, 41
8. Napoleon Hill, Law of Success, Los Angeles, High Roads Media, 2004), 572

Chapter 7

1. Skip Ross with Carole C. Carlson, *Say Yes to Your Potential* (Rockford, MI: Circle "A" Productions, 1983), 145, 146

2. Napoleon Hill, *Think and Grow Rich* (Chatsworth: Wilshire Book Company, 1999), 16

3. Martin Luther King Jr. UBR, Inc., The American, The New Business Magazine For People Who Think. -- http://www.people.ubr.com/

4. Abraham Lincoln, Alan Loy McGinnis, *Bringing Out the Best in People* (Minneapolis: Augsburg Publishing House, 1985), 76.

5. James Allen, 13

6. Malcolm Gladwell, Outliers, New York, Hachette Book Group, 2008), 18

7. Ibid. 18

8. Jordan.htpp://quotations.about.com/od/stillmorefamouspeople/a/michaeljoradan1.html

9. Einstein. http://www.essortment.com/all/biographyofein_rwdi.htm

10. The Civil War Society's "Encyclopedia of the Civil War"http://www.civilwarhome.com/tubmanbio.htm

11. Les Brown, Live Your Dreams, (New York. William Morrow & Company, Inc. 1992), 90

Chapter 8

1. Danforth. I Dare You, 26

2. David Swartz, Magic of Self-Direction, Cornerstone Library, Simon & Schuster, New York, 1982), 12.

3. Kendall White, Critical Issue, Youth Motivation, NASE http://www.self-esteem- nase.org/kendallwhite.shtml.

Chapter 9

1. Mark Fisher/Marc Allen, 107
2. Think Like A Champion, New York, Vanguard Press, 2009), 147
3. T. Harv Eker, Secrets of the Millionaire Mind, New York, Collins Business, 2005), 183
4. Ibid, 183
5. Diana Nightingales' Intro, The Strangest Secret. Strangest Secret Millenium 2000 Gold Recording Audio CD. Earl Nightingale.

<u>Available Services</u>

Consulting and training sessions are available for groups as well as individuals.

For more information contact us via Email: <u>teensuccess101@yahoo.com</u> Or visit us at www. AndrewsLeadershipInternational.com

---

NEED A SPEAKER FOR YOUR EVENT?

Interested in having author John A. Andrews or another speaker from Andrews Leadership International to speak at your event about:

Leadership For EVER

- **EMPOWERMENT**
- **VISION**
- **ENTERTAINMENT**
- **RELATIONSHIPS**

Contact John A. Andrews at <u>john@theteensuccess.com</u>

ABOUT THE AUTHOR

National Bestselling Author John A. Andrews, *screenwriter, producer, and author of several books,* *founded Teen Success in 2009. Its mission statement:* **To** **invigorate and stimulate teens to maximize their full** **potential, to be successful and become contributing** **citizens in the world.** *As an author of books on* *relationships, personal development, and vivid engaging* *stories, John is sought after as a motivational speaker to* *address success principles to young adults. John makes* *an impact in the lives of others because of his passion* *and commitment to make a difference in the world. Being* *a father of three sons propels John even more in his* *desire to see teens succeed. Andrews, a divorced dad of* *three sons ages 14, 12 and 10, was born in the Islands of*

St. Vincent and the Grenadines. He grew up in a home of five sisters and three brothers. He recounts: "My parents were all about values: work hard, love God and never give up on dreams."

Self educated, John developed an interest for music. Although lacking the formal education he later put his knowledge and passion to good use, moonlighting as a disc jockey in New York. This paved the way for further exploration in the entertainment world. In 1994 John caught the acting bug. Leaving the Big Apple for Hollywood over a decade ago not only put several national TV commercials under his belt but helped him to find his niche.

His passion for writing started in 2002, when he was denied the rights to a 1970's classic film, which he so badly wanted to remake. In 2007, while etching two of his original screenplays, he published his first book "The 5 Steps to Changing Your Life" Currently he's publishing his fifteenth volume, while working on empowering teens worldwide.

In 2008 he not only published his second book but also wrote seven additional books that year, and produced the docu-drama based on his second book, Spread Some Love (Relationships 101).

See Imdb: http://www.imdb.com/title/tt0854677/.

UPCOMING RELEASES

Maximize Your Potential
Significance 101

There are things you and I will accomplish in our lifetime that will not only astonish our relatives, friends, neighbors, co-workers but our enemies alike. It has been discovered that 90% of an iceberg rests beneath the surface. It may surprise you that each of us has at least 90% of our potential lying untapped. As human beings, we are known to only use that other 10% of our potential. Like going from good to great, the high achievers in life attain their highest heights by going from success to significance. At this level, their destiny not only embodies greatness but true significance; they add value to others. The well known axiom states: Success is adding value to self, significance is adding value to others. The successful achieves significance by tapping deeper and deeper into their unused capacity.

In my interaction with people of significance, I've discovered that they are not only specialists in their field. At one point in their lives they said **yes** to their potential. As visionaries, they continue to empower others to maximize their God given potential. They realize that they don't have a thousand years to live, so they do all they can with their time, money and skills. They abhor going to their graves with their music leashed.

You too can join the significant by simply saying **yes** to your God given potential.

Junk In The Trunk.

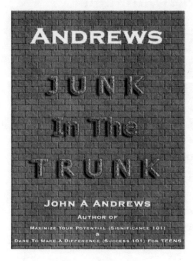

So many people spend a lifetime, looking in their rearview mirror. Their eyes, are focused on all that trash they carry around in the trunk.

This book tells you how to focus on the road, while you get rid of the junk in the trunk.

RELEASES

"QUOTES" Unlimited.

Quotes from my treasury and 101 Quotes Which Inspired Me.

"If we think with a mindset of giving, we entertain abundance, and if we think with an attitude of withholding, we invite lack. As the source gives to the stream so ought the stream to impart to the ocean."

_ John A. Andrews

Quotes From My Treasury.

John A. Andrews

Author of
"Quotes" Unlimited &
How I Wrote 8 Books In One Year™

"If you're still holding on to your accomplishments of yesterday, release your grasp; it's time move on."

_ *John A. Andrews*

The 5 Steps To Changing Your Life

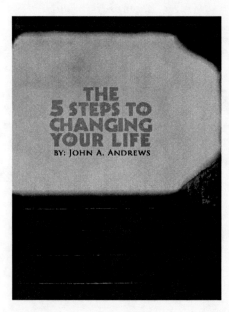

"THE 5 STEPS TO CHANGING YOUR LIFE" In this book , John A. Andrews takes you on a journey from the inside out, extracting insights from his own life and great inspira-tional literature, most of them written seve-ral decades before he was born – delivering nugget after nugget of wisdom - essential for changing your life as well as impacting your world. So many embark upon the task of revolutionizing their home, their church and their world but never start with the "self." Everything you see on the outside first came from within. Real change is an "inside job." Learn the five fundamental steps necessary and pass it on to others.

"SPREAD SOME LOVE (Relationships 101)"

SPREAD SOME LOVE (Relationships 101) was born out of his failed marriage which ended after 13 years in 2000. Since then John has not only read dozens of books on relation-ships but has asso-ciated with several experts on this sub-ject, including Pastors Philip and Holly Wagner, whose marriage is now entering its 24th year. As an entrepreneur and sought after coach, Mr. Andrews believes that marriages should last forever and states: "If a person isn't willing to work on him or herself they should stay out of the falling in love business; the world is full of too many abandoned relationships and broken hearts."

SPREAD SOME LOVE (RELATIONSHIPS 101)

WORKBOOK

Three weeks after the release of the foundation to this workbook "Spread Some Love (Relationships 101)," I was doing a book signing event at a restaurant in Southern California. A woman came up to me and asked if she can scan through my new volume. I enthusiastically gave her the go ahead. Before wrapping the event some two hours later, I noticed that she was not only still holding the book in her hands but was joined by four other women - all in their late 20's to early 30's. I stepped into their space and after introducing myself, joined their huddle. I asked where everyone was in their relationships with a significant other. I learned that two of them were married, two were still single and one was going through a divorce – they weren't very passionate about their relational status.

The woman going through her divorce asked me what motivated me to write such a book. I responded enthusiastically: "Doctors go to school for a reason, so do lawyers, pastors keep studying in order to remain on the pulpit but we fail to work on our relationships on a daily basis. Many of us fall in love and expect that osmosis will pull every-thing together. It doesn't - It can't." She sobbingly echoed: "where were you a year ago." That hit home. A year too late I pondered - her marriage would have been saved. **Writing this workbook was inescapable!**

TOTAL COMMITMENT –
THE MINDSET OF CHAMPIONS

Action is a doing word! Once you acquire this habit, others have no choice but to step aside for you. You are now a crusader, and the world always seems to make way for the person who knows where he or she is going.

HOW I WROTE 8 BOOKS IN ONE YEAR

Writing my first book did not only cause me tap into my unused potential, but brought me off the sidelines and into the game. I decided that no one was going to outwork me. Since I had never taken a typing class, I was not adept at using the computer's keyboard. My word per minute was about a few words a minute. Someone once said: When the dream is big enough the facts don't count. In the summer of 2008, I wrote, published, and released **Spread Some Love (Relationships 101).**

It's my belief that if my thoughts can produce it, it can be written.

CONTACT INFORMATION

For more information about *JOHN A. ANDREWS*, to book speaking engagements, sign up for his mailings, purchase his books and to learn more about other BOOKS THAT WILL ENHANCE YOUR LIFE ™, visit his website at:

www. Theteensuccess.com

EMAIL

john@theteensuccess.com

or

Contact John at:

BOOKS THAT WILL ENHANCE YOUR LIFE™

www.booksthatwillenhanceyourlife.com

NOTES

NOTES

9 780983 141945